Collectors' Coins Great Britain

By Chris Henry Perkins

36th Edition © 2009

ISBN13: 978-0-948964-86-2

Gold Coins	1817 to 1968
Silver Coins	1800 to 2008
Copper Based Coins	1797 to 2008

A wealth of numismatic information and a compilation of averaged selling-prices drawn from the online Rotographic database, dealers' lists, coin auctions, numismatic magazines and experience in the trade. Special thanks to London Coins (www.londoncoins.co.uk) and Colin Cooke (www.colincooke.com) for making their price data available to the author.

The preceding 2008, 35th edition of this book was ISBN13 978-0-948964-76-3.

Errors and Omissions:
Every effort has been made to ensure that the information and price data contained within this book is accurate and complete. However, errors do sometimes have a habit of creeping in unnoticed, and with this in mind the following email address has been established for notifications of omissions and errors: info@rotographic.com. Readers within the UK can also call the telephone number below.

Special thanks to:
Messrs. M Gouby, C King, S P Perkins, M Platt, P R ˙ ˙˙˙˙ˈˈˈˈˈ involved.

This edition is dedicated to Emily Phyllis

D1335891

www.rotographic.
0871 871 5122

In Association with **Predecimal**

DEDICATED TO DECIMALS

The Rotographic title "Check Your Change" contains almost 90 pages just on decimal money! Every single coin type is illustrated and a section on current circulating banknotes is also included. It's all you need to check your coins for rare varieties and your banknotes for that first print run or experimental serial number.

RRP is £5.95 and the book is available from all good book retailers. Quote the ISBN 978-0-948964-80-0.

CONTENTS

INTRODUCTION

This is "Collectors' Coins Great Britain 2009". If this is your first CCGB then welcome to the best value and the most comprehensive British coin book covering British coins from the industrial revolution to the present day. If you already own a previous edition, then thanks very much indeed for your continued patronage.

The cover price of this book has risen slightly to £6.30 from £5.95. It still represents excellent value and is still much cheaper than the nearest rival. The figure of £6.30 was chosen quite deliberately as it happens to be exactly 6 Guineas and I wanted to price a modern book in Guineas just to try to confuse the computers in retail outlets!

For this edition I have gained permission from the British Museum to use a number of images from their 1960 publication: 'English Copper, Tin and Bronze Coins in the British Museum 1558 - 1958'. This is the book usually referred to in the trade simply as 'Peck', after its author, the late Mr C Wilson Peck. The most recent edition of this book is out of print since 1970 and for copper coins (i.e. pre 1860) there is no single more up to date reference work. Most of the images I have used are of variety types and although black and white, they are very clear and should help collectors spot the difference between similar coin types.

This edition benefits from huge amounts of extra price data gleaned from all the auction results of London Coins (in Kent). London Coins are relative new-comers to numismatic auctioning, but despite this they offer some very interesting items and now that a more formal arrangement has been struck, Rotographic receive regular spreadsheets of all the auction results. This extra data helps to keep the pricing accurate.

I've certainly noticed this year that there has been some cooling off in the market. Some coins have gone down slightly in value. I'm not an economist but I'm pretty sure this is down to general lower financial confidence in the world at the moment and collectors simply preferring to spend less - which leads to lower prices, especially at auction. I don't think there's anything to worry about in the long term - there will always remain a hard core collector base even for the very expensive coins and the coins themselves will certainly never become more plentiful! Historically too, coin values have never been as volatile as precious metals, shares and other traditional investments. Another good thing about coins of course is that each is a mini work of art and regardless of the material value, each is a prized possession; so if you want it or need it and can afford it - buy it and enjoy it!

As ever, if you as a reader feel something else could be improved or even if there is something you don't like about this book, please feel free to visit the website, or call the number on the first page to have your say. I want to try to ensure that this book evolves and gets better every year, and I'm grateful for any kind of feedback.

Good luck with your collection or your price research.

Chris Perkins, September 2008

THE LAYOUT
Collectors' Coins Great Britain 2009 is laid out in five sections:

The **Main** section covers the period 1797-1970 and contains the main "Collectors' Coins", that is; all non-proof coins that were issued for circulation and the common mass produced proof coins. This section also covers some of the extremely rare coins of Edward VIII.

The **Gold** section covers Half Sovereigns, Sovereigns, Two Pound Coins and Five Pound coins struck from 1817 to 1968

The **Proof** section contains all the strictly limited proof coins that were never intended for circulation, and most of which are quite rare. This section covers 1797-1967.

The **Maundy** section contains Maundy sets and singles. These were never meant for circulation and are not proofs, so they too have been moved away from the general circulation and proof sections.

The **Decimal** section contains listings of British non gold decimal coins.

HOW TO USE THIS PRICE GUIDE
The first (Main) and second (Gold) sections of this book are arranged in ascending order of face value, starting with the Fractional Farthing and working right up to the gold five pound coin. Each denomination is introduced and the average size and weight data is also specified. Each denomination is arranged in ascending date order, with each change in monarch clearly stated as well as major changes in the coin type.

All listings are split into columns, with a column each for the Date, Reference

MINTAGE FIGURES

It is very important to realise that the mintage figures quoted in this book are very rarely accurate. Until the 1950's the Royal mint did not record the number of coins with a given date, but rather the number of coins struck in a particular year. So for example, the mintage of 1836 Farthings may be quoted as 1,290,240, but it is perfectly possible that a large proportion of those could have been dated 1835 (or even 1837). The mintage numbers do not record the number of coins that for certain types were re-melted either, so don't place any real relevance on the mintage numbers. They are just there to give a general feel for the numbers of coins produced.

INFORMATION ABOUT THE REFERENCE NUMBERS

Throughout this whole book, usually in the second column, you will notice there are reference numbers. The column in which these numbers appear will either be labelled 'PECK', 'FMAN' or 'ESC' and those abbreviations represent the books from which the reference number is taken. Many dealers will quote the numbers in these books when selling coins, as well as the date and condition. Although they are not normally referred to with newer coins. Every pre-decimal non gold coin in this catalogue has been labelled with its reference number from the following publications:

PECK = English Copper, Tin and Bronze Coins in the British Museum 1558-1958, by C Wilson Peck. All the Peck numbers in this book are preceded with a 'P' and all the Copper and Brass coins in this book are cross referenced with the Peck volume. Peck Numbers are sometimes referred to by other publications as 'BMC' (British Musuem Collection).

FMAN = The Bronze Coinage of Great Britain, by Michael J Freeman. This book, which is generally thought of as more up to date with Bronze coinage has been used to provide the reference numbers for all the Bronze coins in this book.

ESC = English Silver Coinage since 1649, by P Alan Rayner. This book has been used to provide reference numbers for all the Silver coins and Cupro-Nickel coins.

It is also important to bear in mind that not all of the coins listed in this book are referred to in the listed reference volumes, and where this is the case the initials **ND** (Not Distinguished) will appear in the reference number column. The initials **MV** are also used in places to indicate that Minor Varieties are in existence.

AN INTRODUCTION TO BRITISH COIN GRADING

The columns containing the market values in this book are headed by 2-4 Standard British coin grade names. Even novice coin collectors will probably realise that coins that are in better than average condition are always worth more than coins that have seen lots of circulation. Grading coins accurately takes a lot of experience in looking at the same types of coins, but, just as a rough idea this is what the grade columns stand for and mean:

Poor: These are not just smooth disks but actually identifiable coins. However, the list of shortcomings can be extensive, ranging from a few letters obliterated in the legend, to coins in which virtually the only detail visible is the date. Very few coins will still retain a value over and above the metal content, but they would need to be pretty rare.

Fair / Good: Heavily worn, but with readable legend and major points of design identifiable. It would be reasonable to say that the vast bulk of 20th century coins in this condition are worth no more than their metal value. Generally speaking, it has never been the practice to produce price data for coins in Fair condition.

F = Fine: Fine coins show considerable wear to all raised surfaces. Some detail should be visible on the designs and some of the main hair volume should be visible on the Monarch's head. Not individual strands, but maybe a parting or signs of head-dress. Many of the coins in your pocket even after just 30 years or less of normal use would probably be Fine or less.

VF = Very Fine: A coin with some wear to the highest areas of the design but which has seen limited circulation. More hair detail is evident and also detail on the other designs. Just as an average guide a coin that has been in normal circulation for approximately 5 years may qualify for VF status.

EF = Extremely Fine: A coin with little sign of being circulated. There may be only the slightest wear to the highest areas and minimal scratches and other marks. Often some of the mint lustre is visible on coins of this grade. As a rough idea a coin in your change would probably be an EF if it had been lucky and was minted just 1 year ago.

(Continued over the page)

AN INTRODUCTION TO BRITISH COIN GRADING (continued)

UNC = Uncirculated: Like the name suggests, the coin should be as it left the mint with no signs of circulation or wear. Not necessarily perfect though, because coins can pick up scratches and what are known as 'bag marks' during mass production and contact with other coins at the mint. The coin should have most of its lustre present and some dealers may expect 100% lustre on coins stated as Uncirculated. An Uncirculated coin would be given to you in your change from a freshly opened bag of new coins. So, as you can imagine, Uncirculated coins that are 30, 60 or even 200 years old, are often pretty rare, and very collectable, hence the higher prices for coins in this grade.

BU = Brilliant Uncirculated: BU is not really an official grade but is increasingly used to refer to an Uncirculated coin with full mint lustre. Such coins are also allowed to exhibit minor signs of mass production.

You may also see the grade FDC which is generally only used when talking about special proof strikings, and it means absolutely perfect in every way.

As well as the basic grades listed here, collectors will often encounter grades like 'GVF' for example. This indicates the coin is not exactly a 'VF' (Very Fine). In fact the 'G' stands for 'Good' so a GVF coin would be better that VF but not quite EF. 'N' stands for 'Near' and 'A' for 'About'. So, the range between VF and EF for example looks like this: VF, GVF, NEF, AEF, EF.

For further information, including images of all coin types in all the collectable grades please see the details of the forthcoming book "The Standard Guide to Grading British Coins" advertised on the opposing page.

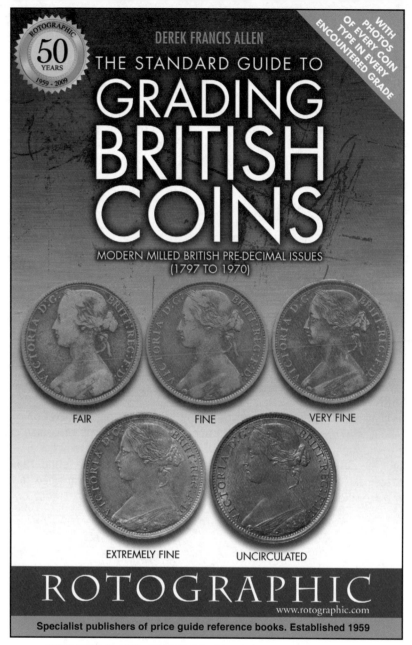

THE STANDARD GUIDE TO GRADING BRITISH COINS

Look out for The Standard Guide to Grading British Coins, also published by Rotographic. It will be ready in early 2009 and will carry the ISBN(13): 978-0-948964-83-1. It will be in hardback format, priced £12.99.

WHERE NO VALUE IS STATED

You will notice that for certain coin types only the higher grade columns are present. This is because these coins are not normally collected in lower grades. But that doesn't mean they are worthless in lower grades. Coins of all grades are there to be collected, and if you want to collect a date run of coins, then the grade doesn't really matter. There are some coins that have missing price data in one or more columns, this usually indicates that no data was available for that coin, in that grade.

SILVER BULLION VALUE

All British silver-coloured coins dated before 1947 contain silver, so even very worn coins are at least worth a few pence. Silver coins dated pre 1920 are .925 (92.5% silver) and coins dated 1920-46 are .500 (50%) silver. The value of silver fluctuates, but generally dealers will gladly pay around 15x face value for all pre 1920 Silver coins, and between 7-8x face value for 1921-46 Silver coins. Bear in mind though, that is decimal face value, so each Threepence has a face value of 1/80th of a GB£ (1.25p). Each Sixpence is 1/40th of a GB£ (2.5p), each Shilling is 1/20th of a GB£ (5p) and each Florin is 1/10th of a GB£ (10p). Halfcrowns are 1/8th of a GB£ (12.5p) and Crowns are a quarter of a GB£, so 25p face value.

MARKETING

It is generally accepted that a dealer's buying price for a coin or collection of coins is about 50-75% of his/her selling price. The precise deal will of course depend on how sought after the items are, and whether the dealer already has a buyer in mind. The dealer is in effect out of pocket until a buyer can be found. The dealer has to make a living, and will only make profit in the long term when the coins can be re-sold.

CLEANING/POLISHING AND HANDLING OF COINS

Do not go anywhere near any coins with any chemicals/abrasives, or anything harder than a soft toothbrush. If your coins are dirty and are low grade, by all means use soap and water and perhaps a toothbrush to remove loose dirt. Make sure they are thoroughly dried, especially copper based coins. High grade coins should ideally be handled by the edges or with gloves, because even the slightest finger print may knock significant value from the coin. If you have a valuable coin with a cosmetic problem, consult an expert first, or simply try to live with it.

VARIETIES / IF IN DOUBT

This book contains the most comprehensive listing of British coin varieties available for all denominations. However, it doesn't list every single variety. Many minute differences would need a whole page to explain, and don't always effect the value of the coins. For this reason some have been left out. If you have any queries about varieties or the contents of this book please consult www.rotographic.com and any important points that are raised will be covered in the next edition.

For further information on coin collecting or buying coins and collecting accessories why not ask at the place you purchased this book. Or if this book was purchased from a book retailer try a google.co.uk search on 'British Coins' or contact Rotographic via email or telephone for information about dealers in your area.

All fractional farthings were originally issued for colonial use. However, half farthings were made legal tender in the United Kingdom from 1842 - 1869. For that reason all fractional farthings have been listed.

Quarter Farthings

The tiny copper quarter farthing was struck solely for use in Ceylon (Sri Lanka). The maundy twopence die was used for the obverse. William Wyon was responsible for creating both the obverse and reverse dies.

VICTORIA Young head. Copper 13.5mm. Weight 1.175g

Date	Peck	Mintage	Fine	VF	EF	UNC/BU
1839	P1608	3,840,000	£10	£35	£60	£75/£90
1851	P1609	Inc below	£20	£50	£150	£220/
1852	P1610	2,215,000	£10	£35	£55	£80/£100
1853	P1612	Inc above	£15	£40	£70	£150/

Victoria 1839 Quarter Farthing

Third Farthings

Third Farthings were made for use in Malta. The farthing was already circulating at a face value of three Maltese grains so the third farthing was made to be exactly a third of the weight of a farthing, thus providing the Maltese with a coin of one grain face value. Obverse and reverse dies were by William Wyon.

GEORGE IV Copper 16mm. Weight 1.567g

Date	Peck	Mintage	Fine	VF	EF	UNC/BU
1827	P1453		£6	£20	£35	£90/

WILLIAM IV Copper 16mm. Weight 1.574g

Date	Peck	Mintage	Fine	VF	EF	UNC/BU
1835	P1477		£8	£20	£50	£120/

VICTORIA Young head. Copper 16mm. Weight 1.564g

Date	Peck	Mintage	Fine	VF	EF	UNC/BU
1844	P1606	1,301,040	£20	£30	£80	£120/
1844	ND	Large 'G'	£20	£35	£120	£220/
1844	P1607	RE instead of REG in legend. UNC: £800 Cooke 2006				
1844	ND. RE instead of REG but thinner flan, 0.88g. AUNC: £650 Cooke 2006					

George IV and William IV Third Farthings. The reverse types were the same.

Victoria 1844 Young head Third Farthing

Third Farthings (continued)

Third farthings from this point onwards were struck in bronze (95% copper, 4% tin and 1% zinc). Not being strictly British, they are not listed in the Freeman reference book, so Peck numbers are quoted instead. Victoria's bust and the reverses are the work of Leonard Charles Wyon, based on a model by W Theed. The portrait of Edward VII was modelled by G W de Saulles, and the portrait of George V by Sir Bertram Mackennal.

VICTORIA Bun head. Bronze 15.5mm. Weight 0.946g

Date	Peck	Mintage	Fine	VF	EF	UNC/BU
1866	P1926	576,000	£4	£10	£15	£40/
1866	ND	No stop after D.G				£60/
1868	P1928	144,000	£5	£10	£20	£45/
1876	P1932	162,000	£4	£15	£25	£50/
1878	P1933	288,000 Large date	£3	£10	£15	£40/
1878	ND	Small date	Scarcer			
1881	P1934	144,000	£3	£8	£12	£50/
1884	P1936	144,000	£3	£5	£12	£40/
1885	P1937	288,000	£3	£6	£10	£40/

EDWARD VII Bronze 15.5mm. Weight 0.957g

Date	Peck	Mintage	Fine	VF	EF	UNC/BU
1902	P2241	288,000	£3	£6	£10	£25/£35

GEORGE V Bronze 15.5mm. Weight 0.931g

Date	Peck	Mintage	Fine	VF	EF	UNC/BU
1913	P2358	288,000	£1	£3	£8	£24/£30

George V 1913 Third Farthing

Half Farthings

The half farthing, like the quarter farthing was originally struck for use in Ceylon (Sri Lanka). Willam Wyon was responsible for the obverse and reverse dies of the three monarchs under which half farthings were struck. The half farthing was made legal tender in the United Kingdom in 1842 and remained so until the demonetization of all the copper coinage in 1869.

GEORGE IV Laureate head. Copper 18mm. Weight 2.35g

Date	Peck	Mintage	Fine	VF	EF	UNC/BU
1828	P1446	7,680,000 Rev A	£25	£60	£130	£200/
1828	P1449	Rev B see below	£15	£40	£100	£250/
1828	ND	As above with large date. AVF: £150				
1830	P1450	8,776,320	£12	£20	£65	£150/
1830	ND	Smaller date	£50	£100	£300	
1830	P1451	Rev B see below	£60	£150	£250	

Rev A: The trident reaches above base of letters.
Rev B: The trident reaches base of letters.

George IV Half Farthing obverse. The reverse type was almost identical to the William IV reverse on the next page.

William IV Copper 18mm. Weight 2.313g

Date	Peck	Mintage	Fine	VF	EF	UNC/BU
1837	P1476	1,935,360	£40	£100	£200	£600/£1000

Victoria Young head, Copper 18mm. Weight 2.365g

Date	Peck	Mintage	Fine	VF	EF	UNC/BU
1839	P1590	2,042,880	£5	£10	£35	£80/£120
1842	P1592		£4	£10	£20	£50/£65
1843	P1593	3,440,640	£3	£8	£15	£50/£125
1844	P1594	6,451,000	£3	£8	£15	£50/£125
1844	P1595	E of REGINA over N	£10	£40	£80	£200/£300
1847	P1596	3,010,560	£4	£7	£25	£50/£90
1847	ND	Last R of BRITANNIA over an A			£70/	
1851	P1597		£4	£12	£40	£100/
1851	ND	1st I over 5	£10	£30	£90	£200/£300
1851	ND	5 struck over blundered number			£55	£75/
1852	P1598	989,184	£6	£12	£40	£75/£130
1853	P1599	955,224	£15	£40	£140	
1854	P1602	677,376	£10	£30	£90	
1856	P1603	913,920		£30	£80	
1856	ND	Large date and letters on Rev. NVF £200, NEF £400, both Cooke 2006				

George IV 1837 Half Farthing

Victoria 1844 Half Farthing

The farthings of 1799, 1806 and 1807 were all struck by Matthew Boulton at his mint in Soho, Birmingham. For the first time ever, a denomination was marked on a British coin, as the 1799 farthing had "1 Farthing" written in the exergue on the reverse. The Boulton Farthing dies were all engraved by Conrad Heinrich Küchler. The Laureate head of George IV was by Benedetto Pistrucci and the reverse by William Wyon.

GEORGE III Copper · 23.5mm. Weight 6.298g

Date	Peck	Mintage	Fine	VF	EF	UNC/BU
1799	P1279	3 Berries in wreath	£4	£12	£30	£80/£150
1799	P1280	4 Berries in wreath	£10	£25	£80	£250/

GEORGE III Copper 21mm. Weight 4.704g

Date	Peck	Mintage	Fine	VF	EF	UNC/BU
1806	P1396	Bust 1	£4	£12	£35	£80/£150
1806	P1397	Bust 2	£4	£10	£30	£80/£150
1806	P1398	Incuse dot on truncation		£50	£100	£200/
1807	P1399	Bust 1	£6	£25	£50	£110/£170

Bust 1: Curls of side whiskers are incuse, and the lower wreath leaves each have overlapping strands of hair. **Bust 2:** Curls are not incuse and the wreath leaves have no overlapping hair.

George III 1799 Farthing

GEORGE IV Laureate Head. Copper 22mm. Weight 4.749g

Date	Peck	Mintage	Fine	VF	EF	UNC/BU
1821	P1407	2,688,000	£2	£7	£40	£70/£100
1821	ND	G over O in GRATIA	£30		£200	
1822	P1409	5,924,352 Obv 1	£2	£7	£25	£60/£100
1822	P1411	Obv 2	£3	£7	£40	£90/
1823	P1412	2,365,440	£3	£12	£40	£90/
1823	P1413	Date has 1 for 1	£12	£60	£150	£270/
1825	P1414	4,300,800 Obv 1	£2	£9	£50	£120/
1825	ND	5 over higher 5	£30		£100	
1825	ND	D of DEI over U	£30	£80	£150	£300
1825	P1415A	Obverse 2	£4	£10	£40	£100/
1826	P1416	6,666,240	£10	£15	£50	£120/
1826	ND	GRATIA R over E	£15	£45	£80	£200/

George III 1806 Farthing

George IV 1822 Farthing

GEORGE IV Bare Head. Copper 22mm. Weight 4.749

Date	Peck	Mintage	Fine	VF	EF	UNC/BU
1826	P1439	Mintage included above	£2	£10	£30	£80/
1826	ND	Roman 1 for 1 (noted 2007)		£150	£300	
1827	P1442	2,365,440	£4	£10	£40	£100/
1828	P1443	2,365,440	£4	£12	£45	£95/£150
1829	P1444	1,505,280	£12	£25	£50	£180/
1830	P1445	2,365,440	£5	£15	£50	£140/£220

George IV 1827 Farthing

1822 and 1825 Obverse varieties.

Obverse 1: The leaf-midribs are single raised lines (left image).

Obverse 2: The 3 lowest leaves have incuse midribs (right image).

When the coin dies became worn, letters that were weak were re-cut using a punch. If the new letter or number was not in exactly the right place this led to the appearance of doubled and sometimes even trebled characters on the coin. This is commonplace during this period, however a major misalignment could add value to the coin.

William IV Copper 22mm. Weight 4.71g

Date	Peck	Mintage	Fine	VF	EF	UNC/BU
1831	P1466	2,68.8,000	£5	£12	£35	£90/£150
1834	P1470	1,935,360 Rev A	£4	£12	£35	£80/£120
1834	P1471	Reverse B	£10	£35	£100	£250/£300
1835	P1472	1,720,320 Rev A	£5	£25	£90	£200/
1835	P1473	Reverse B	£3	£10	£40	£90/
1836	P1474	1,290,240	£9	£20	£50	£120/£160
1837	P1475	3,010,560	£5	£20	£60	£120/£150
1837	ND	7 over 7 (misaligned)		£40	£100	£200/

Reverse A has an incuse line down the arms of the saltire (St Andrews cross).
Reverse B has a raised line down the arms of saltire.

William IV 1837 Farthing.

VICTORIA Young head. Copper 22mm. Weight 4.70g

Date	Peck	Mintage	Fine	VF	EF	UNC/BU
1838	P1553	591,360	£5	£12	£40	£140/
1838*	P1553	DEF. fullstop	£6	£14	£40	£90/£120
1839	P1554	4,300,800	£4	£12	£30	£90/£120
1839	ND	'DEF' no stop	£5	£10	£45	£140/
1839	ND	Two-pronged trident			£200	£300/£400
1840	P1559	3,010,560	£3	£11	£35	£90/
1840	ND	Two-pronged trident				£300/
1840*	ND	'DEF.' variety	£4	£15	£45	
1841	P1560	1,720,320	£4	£10	£35	£100/
1841	ND	Inverted 'V's for 'A's in GRATIA		£200		
1841	ND	As above + dot in 1st 'A' in Britannia VF: £85				
1841	ND	Varieties - REG. and REG for REG:				£100/£150
1842	P1562	1,290,240	£12	£50	£140	£200/
1842	ND	Large '42'	£20	£45	£120	
1843	P1563	4,085,760	£4	£12	£40	£100/£150
1843	P1564	1 for 1 in date			£600	£1100/
1843	ND	3 over 2	£90	£250		
1844	P1565	430,080	£100	£300	£800	£2200/£2500
1845*	P1566	(A)	£5	£15	£50	£110/£170
1845*	ND	3,225,600 (B)	£6	£20	£60	£130/£200
1845	ND	Larger date	£90	£180		
1846	P1567	2,580,480	£12	£40	£100	
1847	P1568	3,879,720	£5	£15	£30	£110/£160
1848	P1569	1,290,246	£5	£20	£65	£150/£200

Victoria 1857 (Young Head) Farthing

*1838 variety DEF. has just one dot where there should be a colon.
*1840 variety DEF.. has two horizontal dots where there should be a colon.
*1845 Type A has a normal straight '8'. Type B has an '8' which leans to the left.

Date	Peck	Mintage	Fine	VF	EF	UNC/BU
1849	P1570	645,120	£35	£90	£250	£400/£550
1850	P1571	430,080 ?	£5	£20	£60	£130/£180
1850	ND	5 over inverted 5 or 3??		£20		£120/
1850	ND	5 over 4		£25	£65	£100/£150
1850	ND	Inverted 'V's for 'A's in Britannia		£150		
1851	P1572	1,935,360	£15	£30	£80	£150/£200
1851	P1573	D of 'DEI' struck over sideways 'D'	£200	£500	£1000/	
1852	P1574	822,528	£30	£70	£200	£325/
1853	P1575	1,028,628 W.W. raised	£2	£5	£50	£120/
1853	ND	3 over 2, raised W.W.		£30	£50	
1853	P1578	WW incuse	£6	£30	£100	£200/
1853	ND	Inverted V's for A's in BRITANNIA. VF:		£110		
1854	P1580	6,504,960	£5	£20	£80	£160/
1855	P1581	3,440,640 WW incuse		£20	£60	£120/
1855	P1582	W.W. raised		£30	£80	£200/
1856	P1583	1,771,392	£7	£20	£80	£160/
1856*	P1584	E over R in Victoria	£70	£150	£500	£800/
1857	P1585	1,075,200	£5	£12	£35	£100/
1858	P1586	1,720,320	£5	£12	£30	£50/£100
1858	ND	Small date	£40	£100		
1859	P1587	1,290,240	£35	£60	£100	£180/
1860	P1588	Obverse date, Cooke 2004 UNC			£5000	
1864	P1589	(Cooke 2000) Colin didn't sell even at			£12,500	

*1856 E/R in VICTORIA. Also described as R over E. Either R was struck over an incorrect E, or E was wrongly selected to improve a poor R; (or ?)

Farthings from this point onwards were struck in bronze (95% copper, 4% tin and 1% zinc until 1923). Bronze was considered better than copper as it was more durable and wore at a slower rate. The coins were also more convenient sizes. The bun head Victorian farthing dies were engraved by Leonard Charles Wyon.

VICTORIA Bun head. Bronze 20mm. Weight 2.84g

Date	FMAN	Mintage	Fine	VF	EF	UNC/BU
BB = Border of Beads. TB = Toothed Border						
1860		2,867,200 with various minor varieties, some rarer:				
1860	496	BB, 3 berries	£3	£10	£30	£90/
1860*	498	Beaded/toothed mule	£150	£400	£600	£1400/
1860	ND	Inverted reverse		[Cooke 2006] £500/		
1860	499	TB, 4 berries	£1	£4	£25	£65/£100
1860	501	TB, 5 berries	£1	£3	£20	£60/£90
1861	502	8,601,600. 4 berries	£2	£6	£25	£70/£100
1861	503	5 berries	£3	£10	£35	£80/£130
1861	ND	Date has small '8'	£2	£4	£12	£55/£80
1862	507	14,336,000	£1	£5	£20	£65/£80
1862	ND	Large fat '8'		£700		
1862	ND	Small '8' over large '8'		£50		
1863	509	1,433,600	£25	£50	£120	£250/
1863	ND	Dot below lighthouse [London Coins 2007]	(Cooke 2006) GVF: £90			£400/£500

Victoria 1860 toothed rim Farthing

Date	FMAN	Mintage	Fine	VF	EF	UNC/BU
1864	511A	2,508,800 serif 4*	£5	£12	£50	£120/
1864	511	plain 4*	£2	£6	£30	£80/£100
1865	512	4,659,200	£2	£5	£20	£60/
1865	513	5 over 2	£3	£8	£40	£120/
1865	ND	5 over 3	£4	£8	£30	£80/
1865	ND	Date has small '8'	£2	£8	£35	£70/
1866	514	3,584,000	£1	£3	£20	£65/£100
1866	ND	RFG for REG (broken die)	£10	£45	£110/
1866	ND	widely spaced 6's	£1	£3	£20	£60/
1867	516	5,017,600	£2	£5	£20	£60/£80
1868	519	4,851,208	£2	£6	£30	£100/£150
1869	522	3,225,600	£15	£50	£200	£380/£480
1872	523	2,150,400	£4	£15	£55	£120/£175
1873	524	3,225,620	£2	£6	£12	£50/£75
1873	ND	Low set 3 in date	£4	£15	£35	£95/£160
1875	528	Large date (5 berries)	£6	£30	£70	
1875	529	Small date (4 berries)	£7	£40	£150	£340/
1875H	530	Small date (5 berries) with Full rose brooch visible on bodice. Extremely Rare, and not to be confused with the very common slightly aged obverse type below. VF: £425				
1874H	525	3,584,000	£2	£6	£28	£90/£150
1874H	527	G's struck over sideways G's GVF: £500 (2006) Fair: £48 (2007 London Coins)				
1875	531	712,760 (for more '1875' details contact Rotographic)				
		Small date, 4 berries	£10	£25	£50	£175/£350
1875H	532	6,092,800, 4 berries	£1	£3	£9	£50/£65
1875H	ND	5 over 2 noted 1999			£50	
1875H	ND*	RF.G for REG	£1	£3	£15	£50/

* A fairly common die break, not strictly a variety.

Date	FMAN	Mintage	Fine	VF	EF	UNC/BU
1876H	534	1,175,200	£5	£10	£30	£70/£100
1876H	534A	Large 6 in date	£10	£25	£60	£100/
1876H	ND*	RF.G for REG die break	£5	£15	£75	£180/£240
1877		Proof Only, see proof section.				
1878	536	4,008,540	£1	£3	£10	£20/£40
1879	538	3,977,180	£4	£10	£30	£80/£120
1879	540	Date has large '9'	£6	£15	£40	£100/
1880	541	1,842,710 (4 berries)	£1	£5	£28	£70/£90
1880	543	(3 berries)	£10	£80	£150	£300/£400
1881	544	4 berries (incl below)		£50		£175/
1881	545-6	3,494,670. 3 berries	£2	£7	£15	£35/£50
1881H	548	1,792,000	£1	£3	£20	£35/£45
1881H	ND	H further to left			£250	
1882H	549	1,790,000	£2	£5	£25	£50/£70
1883	551	1,128,680	£3	£8	£35	£60/£90
1884	553	5,782,000	£1	£2	£4	£15/£30
1885	555	5,442,308	£1	£2	£4	£15/£30
1886	557	7,767,790	£1	£10	£30	£60/£90
1887	559	1,340,800	£1	£4	£25	£55/
1888	560	1,887,250	£1	£4	£25	£50/£60
1890	562	2,133,070	£1	£3	£20	£50/£60
1891	564	4,959,690	£1	£2	£15	£35/£45

*1864 - Plain and serif '4' in date: See the penny section for more details.

'H' centred below date = Heaton Mint (Coin was not made at the Royal Mint)

All Royal Mint coins 1875 to 1878 have an 'R' with a forked tail; the Heaton Mint issues do not. So an 1875 with forked 'R' might well be an 1875H with 'H' removed to Increase value!

During the 35 year run of bun-head farthings, minor changes were occasionally made to age the queens portrait

Minor die varieties of 1881H Farthings occur, but a whole extra book would be needed to point out the intricate but very minor differences!

Date	FMAN	Mintage	Fine	VF	EF	UNC/BU
1892	566	887,240	£5	£10	£30	£75/£100
1893	568	3,904,320	£1	£4	£12	£45/£65
1893	ND	Narrower date	£2	£8	£35	£90/£125
1894	569	2,396,770	£1	£7	£30	£65/£90
1895	570	2,852,853	£10	£20	£50	£100/£150

The veiled head Victoria portrait was engraved by George William de Saulles, from a Model by Thomas Brock. The reverse was also the work of de Saulles. Most of the 1897 farthings, and all farthings up to 1917 were chemically darkened, to avoid them being confused for half sovereigns, which were a very similar size.

VICTORIA Old or widow head. Bronze 20mm. Weight 2.857g

Victoria 1897 Farthing

Date	FMAN	Mintage	Fine	VF	EF	UNC/BU
1895	571	Inc with bun head	£1	£3	£10	£30/£40
1896	572	3,668,610		£2	£8	£25/£35
1897	ND	Bright finish			£15	£40/£60
1897		4,579,800 Blackened.				
1897*	574	Horizon as 1896	£1	£3	£13	£30/£40
1897**	575	Higher horizon	£1	£3	£13	£30/£40
1898	576	4,010,080		£2	£8	£25/£28
1899	577	3,864,616		£1	£8	£40/£55
1900	578	5,969,317		£2	£5	£12/£20
1901	579	8,016,459		£1	£3	£6/£10
1901	ND	Bright finish error				/£55

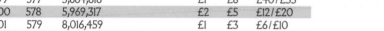

* = The '7' points to a border tooth. ** = The '7' points between two teeth

George William de Saulles was also responsible for the engraving of the dies for the Edward VII farthings. The reverse remained very similar to the last Victorian farthings.

EDWARD VII Bronze 20mm. Weight 2.834g

Date	FMAN	Mintage	Fine	VF	EF	UNC/BU
1902	580	5,125,120. A		£2	£6	£16/£35
1902	ND	Incl above. B		£2	£6	£15/£30
1903	581	5,331,200	£1	£4	£12	£40/£55
1904	582	3,628,800	£1	£4	£9	£18/£30
1904	ND	Bright finish error				£55/
1905	583	4,076,800		£4	£25	£45/
1906	584	5,340,160		£3	£12	£40/£50
1907	585	4,399,360		£2	£10	£20/
1908	586	4,264,960		£4	£12	£40/£55
1909	587	8,852,480		£2	£7	£20/£30
1910	588	2,598,400	£1	£4	£15	£30/£45

All Edward VII Farthings were Chemically darkened and had the Britannia reverse in the same style as old head Victorian farthings. The obverse used the standard portrait of the King.

Type A: Weak strike - patchy breastplate on Britannia.
Type B: Well struck - clear design work.

Farthings of George V, VI and Elizabeth II

The portrait of George V was the work of Sir Bertram Mackennal. The reverse was a slightly altered version of the Edward VII reverse type. The farthings of George VI saw a departure from the traditional designs of former years, and a Wren by H Wilson Parker was chosen to be used as a new reverse type. The George VI portrait was the work of T H Paget. The bust of Elizabeth II was the work of Mary Gillick and the Wren reverse was also used on the Elizabeth II farthings until the last 1956 dated coins.

GEORGE V Bronze 20mm. Weight 2.82lg

Date	FMAN	Mintage	VF	EF	UNC/BU
1911	589	5,196,800 *la	£2	£10	£28/£40
1911	ND	*lb (see right)	£4	£8	£16/£25
1912	590	7,669,760		£4	£12/£16
1913	591	4,134,320		£3	£12/£16
1914	592	6,126,988 BRITT Obv.l		£10	£24/£35
1914	593	BRIT_T (gap)		£10	£20/£30
1915	593A	BRITT (no gap)			£250/£350
1915	594	7,129,254 BRIT_T	£1	£15	£40/
1916	595	10,993,325		£3	£10/
1917	596	21,434,844		£2	£7/
1918	597	19,362,818 Bright			£4/£7
1918	ND	Scarcer, darkened finish		£6	£12/
1919	598	15,089,425		£1	£8/£10
1920	599	11,480,536		£1	£10/£12
1921	600	9,469,097		£1	£9/£11
1922	601	9,956,983		£1	£9/£11
1923	602	8,034,457		£2	£10/£16
1924	603	8,733,414		£1	£8/£10
1925	604	12,634,697		£10	£48/
1926	605	9,792,397		£1	£12/
1927	607	7,868,355		£1	£12/
1928	609	11,625,600		£1	£8/£10
1929	611	8,419,200		£1	£10/£15
1930	613	4,195,200		£1	£10/£12
1931	615	6,595,200		£1	£8/£10
1932	617	9,292,800		£1	£10/£12
1933	619	4,560,000		£1	£8/£10
1934	621	3,052,800		£3	£8/£10
1935	623	2,227,200	£2	£5	£18/£22
1936	625	9,734,400		£1	£5/£7

*1911 - Obv la: Above B.M. the neck is hollow. Obv lb: Above B.M. the neck is flat.

1914 & 1915:
Varieties with different spacing between the T's in BRITT occur. BRITT represents close spacing, and BRIT_T represents far spacing.

George V 1921 Farthing

EDWARD VIII

Date	FMAN	Mintage	UNC/BU
1937	627	Extremely rare £12,000+/ (not issued for general circulation)	

GEORGE VI Bronze 20mm. Weight 2.838g

Date	FMAN	Mintage	UNC/BU
1937	628	8,131,200	£2/£3
1937	629	26,402 Proofs	£5/£8
1938	630	7,449,600	£5/£8
1939	632	31,440,000	£3/£5
1940	634	18,360,000	£3/£5
1941	636	27,312,000	£3/£4
1942	638	28,857,600	£3/£4
1943	640	33,345,600	£3/£5
1944	642	25,137,600	£3/£5
1945	644	23,736,000	£3/£5

George VI 1943 Farthing

GEORGE VI Bronze 20mm. Weight 2.838g

Date	FMAN	Mintage	UNC/BU
1946	646	23,364,800	£3/£5
1947	648	14,745,600	£3/£4
1948	650	16,622,400	£3/£4
1949	652	8,424,000	£3/£5
1950	654	10,324,800	£3/£5
1950	655	17,513 Proofs	£8/£10
1951	656	14,016,000	£3/£6
1951	657	20,000 Proofs	£8/£10
1952	658	5,251,200	£3/£6

Elizabeth II 1954 Farthing. The wren type reverse was also used for the farthings of Elizabeth II

ELIZABETH II Bronze 20mm. Weight 2.852g

Date	FMAN	Mintage	EF	UNC/BU
1953		6,131,037 :		
	660	Obverse 1 Reverse A, From set		£5/£6
	661	Obverse 1 Reverse B	£2	£16/£20
	662	Obverse 2 Reverse A	£3	£15/£25
	663	Obverse 2 Reverse B		£3/£4
	664	40,000 Proofs		£3/£6
	662A	Proof Obverse 2 + Reverse A		£60/£80
1954	665	6,566,400		£1/£2
1955	667	5,779,200		£1/£2
1956	669	1,996,800	£2	£15/£20

Obverse 1: Is poorly defined. The cross points TO a border bead.
Obverse 2: Is sharper. The cross points BETWEEN two border beads.
Reverse A: (uses the dies of George VI) - The 'F' points BETWEEN two beads.
Reverse B: Is similar, but the 'F' points TO a border bead.

1953 Obverse/Reverse Rarity Scale 1 + A is scarce. 2 + A is rare. 1 + B is rare. 2 + B is very common.

Halfpennies

The 1799 halfpenny was the first official halfpenny issue since 1775. Following on from the successful introduction of the Cartwheel Twopence and Penny in 1797, Matthew Boulton also produced the 1799 and 1806/07 Halfpennies. The dies were prepared by Conrad Heinrich Küchler.

GEORGE III Soho Mint, Copper 31mm. Weight 12.659g

Date	Peck	Mintage	Fine	VF	EF	UNC/BU
1799	P1248	5 incuse ship gunports	£8	£25	£50	£100/
1799	P1249	6 raised ship gunports	£8	£25	£70	£120/
1799	P1250	9 raised ship gunports	£8	£30	£80	£120/
1799	P1251	Plain ship hull	£9	£30	£80	£130/
1799	P1252	Raised line on ship, no guns	£9	£25	£80	£130/

2nd type, Soho Mint, Copper 29mm. Weight 9.428g

Date	Peck	Mintage	Fine	VF	EF	UNC/BU
1806	P1376	Olive branch no berries	£5	£18	£50	£90/£150
1806	ND	Ball under trident prongs, which is normally only seen on the proof varieties. Reported on predecimal.com 2006.				
1806	P1377	3 berries 'SOHO' *	£5	£20	£55	£80/
1807	P1378	3 berries 'SOHO' *	£5	£20	£55	£80/

* The word SOHO is underlined on the reverse of the coin.

1799 Soho Halfpenny

1806 Soho Halfpenny

The copper halfpennies of George IV, William IV and Victoria are all the work of William Wyon (although the portrait of William IV was based on a model by Sir Francis Chantry). The reverse type remained the same until REG replaced REX for the issues struck under Queen Victoria.

GEORGE IV Laureate head, Copper 28mm. Weight 9.337g

Date	Peck	Mintage	Fine	VF	EF	UNC/BU
1825	P1431	215,040	£10	£40	£90	£175/
1826	P1433	9,031,630, Rev A	£6	£25	£70	£120/
1826	P1436	Rev B	£8	£30	£60	£120/
1827	P1438	5,376,000	£9	£30	£70	£160/

1826: Rev A: The saltire of shield has two incuse lines. Rev B: The saltire of shield has one raised line.

The saltire/St. Andrew's cross, is often divided by lines. More info about the St.Andrews cross and similar varieties can be found in the George IV penny section.

WILLIAM IV Bare head, Copper 28mm. Weight 9.389g

Date	Peck	Mintage	Fine	VF	EF	UNC/BU
1831	P1461	806,400	£12	£25	£60	£150/
1834	P1464	537,600	£12	£25	£60	£150/
1837	P1465	349,400	£12	£30	£80	£180/
1837	ND	Small date over large			£90	

VICTORIA Young head with date below, Copper 28mm. Weight 9.457g

Date	Peck	Mintage	Fine	VF	EF	UNC/BU
1838	P1522	456,960	£6	£10	£50	£130/
1841	P1524	1,075,200	£5	£10	£40	£110/
1841	ND	Broken die: DEI reads DF.I			£40	(2002)
1841	ND	Alignment Up/down (Ap I)	£9	£25	£100	£225/
1843	P1527	967,680			£35	£80
1844	P1528	1,075,200	£15	£30	£80	£140/
1845	P1529	1,075,200	£40	£90	£275	£350/
1846	P1530	860,160	£15	£30	£80	£140/
1847	P1531	752,640	£5	£15	£50	£100/
1848	P1533	322,560	£10	£30	£100	£270/

George IV 1826 Halfpenny

William IV 1837 Halfpenny

On the next page some of the 1850s halfpennies have either no dots near the shield (left image) or 7 incuse dots on and around the shield (right image)

VICTORIA Young head with date below, Copper 28mm. Weight 9.457g

Date	Peck	Mintage	Fine	VF	EF	UNC/BU
1848	P1532	8 struck over 7	£6	£20	£90	£200/
1848	ND	8 struck over 3	£5	£20	£90	
1851	P1534	215,040 no dots on				
		or above shield		£20	£45	£100/
1851	P1535	Shield, 7 incuse dots	£6	£20	£60	£140/
1852	P1536	637,056 (no dots)	£5	£16	£45	£100/
1852	P1537	Shield, 7 incuse dots	£6	£18	£70	£130/
1853	P1539	1,559,040	£5	£10	£40	£80/
1853	P1538	3 over 2	£8	£22	£60	£150/
1854	P1542	12,354,048 ?	£5	£12	£40	£80/
1855	P1543	1,455,837	£5	£12	£40	£80/
1856	P1544	1,942,080	£7	£20	£55	£120/
1856	ND	6 over larger 6 (values perhaps a little more than above)				
1857	P1545	Shield, 7 incuse dots	£5	£20	£60	£150/
1857	P1546	1,182,720 (no dots)	£7	£30	£90	£200/
1858	P1549	2,472,960	£5	£15	£50	£90/
1858	ND	Smaller date	£5	£15	£50	£90/
1858	P1547	Last 8 over 6	£5	£15	£40	£80/
1858	P1548	Last 8 over 7	£5	£15	£40	£90/
1859	P1551	1,290,340	£10	£30	£70	£150/
1859	P1550	9 struck over 8	£6	£20	£60	£120/
1860*	P1552	Extremely rare	£200	£500	£2750	£4000/

*Copper type - Date is below head, not below Britannia.

Victoria 1853 Halfpenny

In 1860 the first bronze halfpennies were produced in line with the bronze alloy used for the farthings and pennies. The dies were the work of Leonard Charles Wyon. Massive demands were made on the Royal Mint and as a result of this some coins were struck by private mints in Birmingham to ease the workload.

VICTORIA 'Bun' head, date on reverse, Bronze 26mm. Weight 5.693g
Beaded Borders:

Date	FMAN	Mintage	Fine	VF	EF	UNC/BU
1860	258	Obv 1	£3	£10	£35	£80/£150

(Freeman 258 has 2 slightly different reverses, distinguishable by the differences in the length of Britannia's hair)

1860	260A	Obv 1*			£35	
1860	260C	Mule toothed/beaded borders (Coincraft 1995) £1000				

Toothed borders:

Date	FMAN	Mintage	Fine	VF	EF	UNC/BU
1860	261	Obv 2, Rev B	£2	£8	£35	£90/£140
1860	264	Obv 2, Rev C	£2	£8	£35	£90/£140
1860	265	Obv 3, Rev B	£2	£8	£40	£90/£150
1860	266	Obv 4, Rev B	£4	£12	£40	£90/£140
1860	267	Obv 4, Rev C			£120	£200/
1860	ND	F of HALF over P	£250			

1861 - 12 minor varieties occur, most dealers do not distinguish.
See also proof halfpennies in the proof section.

Date	FMAN	Mintage	Fine	VF	EF	UNC/BU
1861	269-82	54,118,400	£3	£8	£50	£150/
1861	274A/82A	6 over 8	£1000 (Fine)			
1861	279	Last 1 over lower 1 reported on predecimal.com forum.				
1861	ND	R over B in BRITT. See illustration on the following page.				

Obv 1 has 6 berries in the wreath arranged in pairs. Obv 1* is as Obv 1 with minor changes - the knot in the hair tie has been removed. Obv 2 has 7 berries. Obv 3 has 5 berries. Obv 4 has 4 berries.

Reverse types: B - lighthouse tapering, pointed. C - lighthouse cylindrical with rounded top. Some 1860 Bun head Halfpennies bear F's with little or no lower serif to the lower horizontal bar.

1861 Halfpenny detail showing the R over B in BRITT. First made public on the Predecimal.com forum in 2006 by Gary Brett.

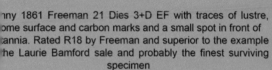

VICTORIA 'Bun' head

Date	FMAN	Mintage	Fine	VF	EF	UNC/BU
1862	289	61,107,200	£2	£6	£25	£65/£110
1862	288	B to left of Lighthouse. VG: £260 (2006)				
1862	288A	C to left of Lighthouse				£2000+?
1862	290A	Unbarred A left of lighthouse. AUNC: £1600 (2008)				
1863	292	15,948,800	£2	£12	£35	£160/
1863	294	With smaller straighter '3'.	£25			£120/
1864	295	537,600	£8	£20	£70	£185/
1865	296	8,064,000	£20	£60	£160	
1865	297	5 over 3	£35	£95	£200	£360/£450
1866	298	2,508,800	£10	£20	£60	£120/
1867	300	2,508,806	£10	£25	£80	£160/
1868	303	3,046,400	£10	£20	£60	£140/
1869	306	3,225,600	£15	£50	£250	£460/
1870	307	4,350,739	£8	£25	£70	£150/
1871	308	1,075,280 ?	£20	£50	£175	£350/£480
1872	309A	4,659,410	£5	£10	£60	£150/
1873	310	3,404,880	£5	£12	£60	£175/
1873	311	Upper and lower arms of St. Andrews cross slightly out of line with each other.			£120	
1874	312-317	1,347,665 16 Wreath leaves	£10	£32	£75	£200/
1874H	318	5,017,600	£5	£22	£50	£120/
1875	321-322A	5,430,815. MV	£5	£22	£50	£120/
1875H	323	1,254,400	£5	£20	£50	£120/
1876H	325-329	6,809,600. MV	£5	£20	£50	£130/
1877	330-334	5,209,505. MV	£5	£18	£40	£110/£180
1878	334/5/7	1,425,535. MV	£10	£30	£90	£200/£300
1879	338/9	3,582,545. MV	£6	£20	£60	£140/
1880	340/41A	2,423,465. MV	£2	£5	£30	£120/
1881	342/43A	2,007,515. MV	£4	£8	£30	£120/
1881H	344	1,792,000	£4	£8	£30	£120/
1882H	347	4,480,000	£4	£8	£30	£120/
1883	349	3,000,725. Brooch*	£4	£8	£30	£120/
1883	348/348A/351	Rose*. MV		£20	£65	£140/

Victorian Bun head 1888 Halfpenny

MV = Minor varieties exist. Varieties not generally distinguished by most dealers and specialist reading is required for further identification details.

*1863 - Varieties in the style of the '3' in the date. One has a larger upper section and both are thought to exist in approximately equal numbers.
*1883 - At the Queen's neckline is either a small brooch or a small rose. The brooch consists of a large oblong shape with 6 ovals surrounding it.

VICTORIA 'Bun' head, date on reverse, Bronze 26mm. Weight 5.693g

Date	FMAN	Mintage	Fine	VF	EF	UNC/BU
1884	352	6,939,580	£4	£8	£30	£90/
1885	354	8,600,574	£4	£8	£30	£90/
1886	356	8,586,155	£4	£8	£30	£80/
1887	358	10,701,305	£2	£6	£25	£80/
1888	359	6,814,070	£2	£6	£25	£80/
1889	360	7,748,234	£1	£5	£35	£80/
1889	361	9 over 8	£8	£30	£100	£230/
1890	362	11,254,235	£1	£6	£15	£55/
1891	364	13,192,260	£1	£5	£12	£55/£65
1892	366	2,478,335	£2	£6	£20	£75/
1893	368	7,229,344	£1	£5	£20	£70/
1894	369	1,767,635	£3	£10	£40	£125/

VICTORIA Old or widow head. Bronze 26mm. Weight 5.644g

The obverse for this issue was engraved by George William de Saulles from a model by Thomas Brock, whose initials appear under the shoulder. The reverse is a modified version of the Leonard Charles Wyon design, with the lighthouse and ship removed.

Date	FMAN	Mintage	Fine	VF	EF	UNC/BU
1895	370	3,032,154	£1	£3	£10	£30/£40
1896	371/2	9,142,500. MV	£1	£2	£10	£25/£40
1897	374	8,690,315	£1	£2	£10	£25/£35
1897	373	Higher tide *	£2	£4	£15	£35/£40
1898	375	8,595,180	£1	£3	£15	£30/£35
1899	376	12,108,001	£1	£3	£10	£25/£35
1900	377	13,805,190	£1	£2	£10	£25/£35
1901	378	11,127,360	£1	£2	£8	£20/£25

* The 1897 higher tide variety has a tide level with the folds in Britannia's robe. The normal tide type has a tide level with the bottom of the robe. The veiled head Victorian Halfpenny was very similar in style to the penny.

EDWARD VII Britannia Reverse, Bronze 26mm. Weight 5.67g

The obverse of this issue was also engraved by George William de Saulles. Initially the same reverse was used as previously.

Date	FMAN	Mintage	Fine	VF	EF	UNC/BU
1902	380	Low tide,	£9	£30	£70	£140/
1902	381	13,672,960 High tide		£2	£8	£25/£35
1903	382	11,450,880		£2	£15	£40/£50
1904	383	8,131,200	£3	£6	£15	£45/£60
1905	384	10,124,800		£4	£20	£45/£55
1906	385	11,101,440		£3	£12	£30/£50
1907	386	16,849,280		£3	£12	£30/£50
1908	387	16,620,800		£3	£12	£30/£40
1909	388	8,279,040		£4	£15	£30/£40
1910	389	10,769,920		£2	£10	£35/£50

The Low Tide variety referred to above and in the Edward VII penny section may be determined thus: if the horizon meets Britannia at the point below the knee, where right and left legs cross; NORMAL tide is indicated. If, however, the horizon meets Britannia at a much lower point - nearer the hem of her drape - then a LOW TIDE variety has been detected. Comparison with a normal tide other date Edward VII coin makes it much easier to tell.

1905 Halfpenny

The BM initials on the truncation of George V stand for Bertram Mackennal, the designer of the George V bust. The first reverse type was identical to that used for Edward VII. Unlike the pennies, there are no 'H' or 'KN' halfpennies, instead, many of the blanks produced for George V halfpennies were made by private firms in Birmingham. There were problems with 'ghosting' (the faint outline of one side appearing on the other side) for this issue throughout most of the reign. Despite the bronze alloy being changed in 1923 (to 95.5% copper, 3% tin and 1.5% zinc) and the head being modified in 1925, this problem was not completely solved until the issue of the smaller head type in 1928.

GEORGE V Britannia Reverse, Bronze 26mm. Weight 5.658g

Date	FMAN	Mintage	VF	EF	UNC/BU
1911		12,570,880			
	390	*Obverse 1a	£2	£7	£25/£35
1911	ND	*Obverse 1b	£3	£8	£25/£35
1912	391	21,185,920	£2	£8	£28/£35
1913	392	17,476,480	£2	£8	£28/£40
1914	393	20,289,111	£2	£8	£28/
1915	394	21,563,040	£5	£12	£35/
1916	395	39,386,143	£1	£8	£30/
1917	396	38,245,436	£1	£8	£30/£40
1918	397	22,321,072	£1	£8	£30/£40
1919	398	28,104,001	£1	£8	£30/£45
1920	399	35,146,793	£1	£8	£28/£35
1921	400	28,027,293	£1	£8	£28/£35
1922	401	10,734,964	£2	£8	£28/£40
1923	402	12,266,282	£1	£8	£28/£40
1924	403	13,971,038	£1	£10	£30/£40
1925	404	12,216,123 Head as For 1924	£1	£6	£30/£40
1925	405	Modified effigy as for 1926, see appendix 1			
			£3	£8	£35/£50
1926	406	6,712,306	£2	£6	£30/£40
1927	408	15,589,622	£1	£6	£25/£35
Smaller Head:					
1928	410	20,935,200	£1	£5	£24/£30
1929	412	25,680,000	£1	£14	£50/£65
1930	414	12,532,800	£1	£6	£20/£28
1931	416	16,137,600	£1	£6	£20/£28
1932	418	14,448,000	£1	£5	£18/£22
1933	420	10,560,000	£1	£5	£20/£25
1934	422	7,704,000	£1	£6	£24/£30
1935	424	12,180,000	£1	£3	£15/£22
1936	426	23,008,800	£1	£3	£12/£20

1911* Obverse 1a has a hollow neck.
Obverse 1b has a flat neck.

1911 & 1912: Some dies were punched with date close to line of exergue.
Small gap = Rev A.
Clear gap = Rev B.

Combinations:: 1a+A 1a+B 1b+A 1b+B.

Most dealers do not differentiate.

George V Halfpenny 1913

George V Halfpenny 1931
(Smaller head and modified Britannia)

EDWARD VIII Reverse Golden Hind ship, Bronze 26mm
1937   Excessively rare, impossible to value.

As with the farthings of George VI, the decision was taken to break from tradition and change the reverse on the halfpennies too. Both the obverse and reverse were designed by Thomas Humphey Paget, whose initials appear to the right of the Golden Hind on the reverse.

GEORGE VI Reverse Golden Hind ship, Bronze 26mm. Weight 5.7g

Date	FMAN	Mintage	EF	UNC/BU
1937	429	24,504,000	£1	£5/£6
1937	430	26,402 proofs		£5/£6
1938	431	40,320,000	£1	£8/£9
1939	433	28,924,800	£1	£10/£12
1940*	437/8	32,162,400	£2	£9/£12
1940	435	Thin rim, short teeth		£10/£16
1941	439	45,120,000	£1	£8/£9
1942	441	17,908,800	£1	£5/£6
1943	443	76,200,000	£1	£8/£8
1944	445	81,840,000	£1	£5/£6
1945	447	57,000,000	£1	£5/£6
1946	449	22,725,600	£2	£8/£9
1947	451	21,266,400	£1	£5/£6
1948	453	26,947,200	£1	£5/£6

*1940: 3 varieties -
Type 1: 'L' points between beads and the 'P' points to a bead. Type 2: 'L' and 'P' point between beads. Type 3: The 'L' points to a bead (see 'Pointings', appendix 1)

These varieties are rarely distinguished, and the prices are usually the same for each.

From 1949 the title IND:IMP (Emperor of India) was removed due to the India of the British Raj becoming two independent states (India and Pakistan).

Date	FMAN	Mintage	EF	UNC/BU
1949	455	24,744,000	£1	£7/£8
1950	457	24,153,600	£2	£10/£12
1950	458	17,513 Proofs FDC	£12	
1951	459	14,868,000	£3	£14/£16
1951	460	Proofs 20,000 FDC	£10	
1952	461	33,278,400	£2	£20/£30

George VI Halfpenny 1945

Elizabeth II 1959 Halfpenny

The Golden Hind vessel was continued as the reverse type on the Halfpennies of Elizabeth II. Mary Gillick designed the obverse portrait, and her initials appear on the centre of the truncation of the shoulder. The first coins issued in 1953 had a very low relief portrait and showed very little detail, particularly in the hair area. The obverse die was re-cut during 1953, leading to the two slight varieties for that year. In 1954 the BRITT:OMN (of all the Britons) title was removed due to the changing state of the fading British Empire.

ELIZABETH II Reverse Golden Hind ship, Bronze 26mm. Weight 5.658g

Date	FMAN	Mintage	EF	UNC/BU
1953		8,910,000:		
1953	463	Obverse 1		£3/£5
1953	464	Obverse 2		£1/£2
1953	465/A	40,000 Proofs. MV		£3/£6
1954	466/8	19,375,200.MV	£6	£25/£35
1955	469	18,465,600		£4/£5
1956	471-5	21,799,200.MV		£5/£6
1957	477	39,672,000		£2/£3
1957*	476	Calmer sea rev	£6	£25/£40
1958	479/80	66,331,200. MV		£2/£3
	481	Thicker rim, shorter teeth		£150/ (consult author!)
1959	483	79,176,000		£2/£3
1960	485	41,340,000		£4/£5
1962	487	41,779,200		£2/£3
1963	489	42,720,000		£2/£3
1964	491	78,583,200		£1/£2
1965	492	98,083,200		£1/£2
1965	ND	Error N.Zealand Rev		£450
1966	493	95,289,600		50p/£1
1967*	494	146,490,400 Normal rim		40p/80p
1967*	495	Wide rim BU 2007		/£2.00 (Predecimal.com)
1970	495A/B.	750,424 Proofs		MV/£3.50 (Predecimal)

*Total mintage for 1967 Includes 46,226,400 struck in 1968, dated 1967.

1953 - Obv 1: The lower relief head. The cross points between rim beads. Obv 2: Slightly sharper. The Cross points to a rim bead.

1967 - Wide Rim or normal rim:

The illustration above shows both rim types. Without a comparison the difference can be detected by looking at the 'I' in 'DEI'. The wide rim variety 'I' points between two rim beads with the normal rim coin it points directly at a rim bead.

The top image to the right is the 1957 Calm sea variety. The bottom image is the normal 1957 with choppy sea.

Minor reverse varieties occur for the 1957 calm sea type:
1. The '7' points to a bead. 2. The '7' points to left of bead. 3. The '7' points to space. 4. A blunter '7' that points to a bead. Number 2 is thought to be the rarest.

From 1770 until the end of the 18th Century the practice of melting down the official copper coins and making lightweight forgeries had become so widespread that it prompted industrialist Matthew Boulton to offer a potential solution. He proposed that each coin should actually be made to contain its value in copper and that the quality should be improved by using a retaining collar during striking (to give a perfectly round coin) and by designing the coins with thick raised borders to prevent them wearing so easily. Conrad Heinrich Küchler was the designer. By 1806 the price of copper had risen, and as a result the second Soho penny type was made of reduced weight. In fact, by the time they were ready, the price of copper had fallen and the intrinsic weight was less than the face value. The public accepted this, and ever since then the intention has been to make coins with an actual metal value less than the face value. It is perhaps a strange coincedence that exactly 200 years later the opposite should happen. In 2006, a steep rise in the price of copper due to the demand from China and India, caused the value in existing modern bronze 1p's and 2p's to be worth more than the face value of the coins. I expect Mr Boulton would find it quite amusing that after 200 years the fluctuations in the price of copper could still make the mintmaster sweat!

George III 1797 Penny

* Varieties for 1797 concern the number of leaves in the Kings headdress.

GEORGE III First Soho 'Cartwheel' type, Copper 36mm. Weight 1oz/28.35g (official)

Date	Peck	Mintage	Fine	VF	EF	UNC/BU
1797	P1132	10 leaves*	£11	£40	£200	£340/
1797	P1133	11 leaves*	£11	£50	£200	

George III 1806 Penny

GEORGE III Second Soho type, Copper 35mm. Weight 18.876g

Date	Peck	Mintage	Fine	VF	EF	UNC/BU
1806	P1342	Type A*	£8	£25	£65	£190/£320
1806	P1343	Type B*	£5	£20	£55	£160/
1807	P1344		£8	£20	£55	£190/£300
1808	P1346	One Known		Spink 1985		£15,000
1808	"			Coincraft 1996		£35,000

* 1806 - Type A (above left) has a small incuse hair curl to the right of the tie knot. Type B (above right) has a slightly different pattern of curls.

George IV 1826 Penny

GEORGE IV Copper 34mm. Weight 18.72g.

Date	Peck	Mintage		Fine	VF	EF	UNC/BU
1825	P1420	1,075,200	Type A	£15	£40	£130	£290/
1826	P1422	5,913,000	Type A	£12	£30	£100	£290/
1826	P1425	Inc above.	Type B	£12	£40	£100	£290/
1826	P1427	Inc above.	Type C	£15	£45	£130	£290/
1827	P1430	1,451,520	Type A	£150	£400	£1250	£2500/

No pennies or halfpennies were issued from 1820 to 1824, and it was only when the new portrait by William Wyon was designed in 1825 (which the king much preferred) that an issue of pennies and halfpennies was made. The reverse was also the work of William Wyon.

Type A   Type B   Type C

The reverse varieties of the 1826 George IV pennies all concern slight differences to the cross of St. Andrew in the flag on the shield:

Rev A = No central line along arms of cross.
Rev B = Thin, raised line along cross.
Rev C = Thick, broad raised line along cross.

With many worn coins these varieties are impossible to spot, especially without a comparison.

William IV 1837 Penny

The portrait of King William IV was engraved by William Wyon, from a bust by Sir Francis Chantrey. The reverse was the same as that used for King George IV. Coins were also struck in 1832, 1835 and 1836, but were not dated as such.

WILLIAM IV Copper 34mm. Weight 18.85g

Date	Peck	Mintage	Fine	VF	EF	UNC/BU
1831	P1455	806,400 no WW	£15	£50	£250	£400/£425
1831	ND	WW with no Dots	£35			
1831	P1458	.W.W incuse on trunc	£25	£80	£175	£400/£500
1831	P1458	W.W incuse on trunc	£150			
1834	P1459	322,560	£25	£65	£300	£700/
1837	P1460	174,720	£60	£150	£650	£1000/

trunc = truncation, the base of the monarch's neck.

The copper Victorian pennies were, like the previous, engraved by William Wyon, who was clearly kept quite busy by the relatively frequent change of British monarchs in the first half of the 19th Century. The only change to the reverse was to replace 'REX' with 'REG' (for Regina).

VICTORIA Young Head, date below head, Copper 34mm. Weight 18.82g

Date	Peck	Mintage	Fine	VF	EF	UNC/BU
1841	P1480	913,920 REG:	£10	£50	£200	£350/
1841	P1484	No colon REG	£5	£15	£55	£80/
1843	P1486	483,830 colon REG:	£200			
1843	P1485	No colon REG	£70	£450	£700	£800/£1000
1844	P1487	215,040	£8	£18	£50	£100/£150
1845	P1489	322,560	£40	£200		
1846	P1490	483,840 DEF_:	£30	£100		
1846	P1491	DEF:	£50	£200		
1847	P1492	430,080 DEF:	£7	£25	£80	£150/
1847	P1493	DEF_:	£7	£25	£65	£100/£200
1848	P1496	161,280	£7	£25	£45	£110/£200
1848	P1494	8 over 6	£10	£30	£130	£220/
1848	P1495	8 over 7	£7	£20	£70	£150/
1849	P1497	268,800	£300	£600	£2000	
1851	P1498	432,224 DEF_:	£10	£30	£100	£230/£300
1851	P1499	DEF:	£14	£25	£85	£120/£200
1853	P1500	1,021,440 DEF_:	£5	£12	£40	£80/£100
1853	ND	Narrow date		£50	£100/	
1853	P1503	DEF:	£4	£15	£50	£100/
1853	P1504	PT	£20	£35	£70	£120/

The copper Victorian pennies were, like the previous, engraved by William Wyon, who was clearly kept quite busy by the relatively frequent change of British monarchs in the first half of the 19th Century. The only change to the reverse was to replace 'REX' with 'REG' (for Regina).

VICTORIA Young Head, date below head, Copper 34mm. Weight 18.82g

Date	Peck	Mintage	Fine	VF	EF	UNC/BU
1854	P1505	4 over 3	£15	£45	£100	£150/
1854	P1506	6,720,000 PT	£5	£18	£50	£100/
1854	P1507	OT	£5	£20	£60	£100/
1855	P1508	5,273,866 OT	£5	£15	£60	£100/
1855	P1509	PT	£7	£20	£50	£100/
1856	P1510	1,212,288 DEF: PT	£40	£120	£350	£900/
1856	P1512	DEF_: OT	£30	£100	£700	£2000/
1857	P1514	752,640 DEF: PT	£8	£30	£70	£120/
1857	P1513	DEF_: OT	£5	£15	£50	£90/
1857	P1514	Smaller date PT	£5	£15	£50	£90/
1858		1,559,040:				
	P1515	2nd 8 over 3		£60	£160	£300/
	ND	2nd 8 over 6		£60		
	P1516	2nd 8 over 7		£10	£70	£140/
	ND	2nd 8 over 9	(noted 2003)		£85/	
	P1517	Smaller date	£4	£10	£50	£130/£170
	P1518	Large date, no W.W.	£4	£10	£40	£170/£300
	ND	Large date over small date. VF: £36 (noted 2008)				
1859	P1519	1,075,200 Large date	£8	£25	£80	£170/
1859	ND	9 over 8	£6	£16	£100	£180/
1859	P1519	Smaller date	£8	£30	£100	£190/
1860*	P1521	60 struck over 59	£1500			

*NOT date below Britannia smaller bronze type.

Victoria 1853 Penny

DEF: = near colon
DEF_: = far colon
OT - ornamental trident
PT - plain trident

Plain trident coins have near colons.

From 1839 to 1851 all have Ornamental tridents.

An ornamental trident (right image) is shown in comparison to a Plain trident (left image). Notice the extra garnishing under the main prongs of the ornamental trident.

The images above also illustrate a near colon after DEF and the far colon (right image)

The 'Bun' Penny

Copper, when alloyed with small quantities of tin and zinc produces bronze, which is a tougher metal. This metal was used (and is still used) to produce british 'coppers' from 1860 onwards. The dies of these lighter, smaller pennies were engraved by Leonard Charles Wyon, a son of William Wyon, who was clearly born to take over from his father (he was actually born on the Royal Mint premises in 1826).

The early bun head series is probably the most complicated coin series ever! As you can see, there are 17 different types for the circulation 1860 coin alone. Correct identification can be a problem with coins in lower grades. Illustrations of every single type would be beyond the scope of this book and readers are refered to 'The British Bronze Penny - Struck for use as currency 1860 - 1970' by Michael Gouby. The book is available on his website: www.michaelcoins.co.uk

The reverse type letters are strictly those specified by Freeman in 'The Bronze Coinage of Great Britain". Here is a brief outline of the major reverse types:

Reverse A = The crosses are outlined by close, double raised lines, Britannia's thumb does not touch cross. no rock to left of lighthouse. **Reverse B** = The crosses are outlined with treble incuse lines, Britannia's thumb touches cross of St. George, no rock to left of lighthouse. **Reverse C** = Similar to Rev. A, but cross outlines are thinner and wider apart. Small rock to the left of lighthouse. **Reverse D** = As Reverse C, but with minor modifications to rocks and sea and, of course, a toothed border. **Reverse E** = As Reverse D, but with L.C.W. incuse below the foot, and the rim of the shield is thicker. **Reverse F** = No L.C.W signature and a rounded top to the lighthouse. Reverse G = No L.C.W signature. The shield is slightly convex (all previous types are flat). Where the letter 'H' appears in the listings after the date, it indicates a Heaton mint coin, distinguished by a small 'H' under date of the coin.

Victoria 1862 Penny
in fairly low grade

The varieties and design of the Bronze Victorian pennies are described in exquisite detail, by Michael J. Freeman in his book 'The Bronze Coinage of Great Britain' and by Michael Gouby in his book 'The British Bronze Penny - Struck for use as Currency 1860 - 1970'.

Above is Reverse A. Note the double raised lines outlining the crosses and that Britannia's thumb doesn't touch the cross.

Reverse B. Note the treble raised lines outlining the crosses and that Britannia's thumb does touch cross.

VICTORIA Bun Head, date below Britannia, Bronze 30.81mm. Weight 9.442g
1860 Bronze Penny. Mintage: 5,053,440
Beaded rim (TI), Obverse: 'L.C.WYON' partly on truncation

Rev	FMAN	Mintage	Fine	VF	EF	UNC/BU
A	1		£80	£300	£900	
A	ND	extra heavy flan (probably a proof)		£750		
B	6		£40	£100	£220	£500/
C	7		£100		£500	£1200
Mule	8	bead obv/tooth rev. Fine: £1100. GEF £2900				
Mule	9	tooth obv/bead rev. Fine: £700. EF w/lustre £2700				
D	13	signature below shield		£20	£100	£320/
E	14	signature below foot		£200	£600	£1000/
D	10	signature below shield		£15	£70	£180/£250
D	ND	N of ONE over sideways N			£200+	£1000/
D	ND	struck on heavy flan		£250		
D	15	signature below truncation		£20	£100	£200/
D	16	no signature 15 leaves		£50	£200	£500/
D	17	no signature 16 leaves		£50	£250	£600/
D	ND	ONF PENNY variety: damaged 'E':				
			£12	£45	£175	£375/
	ND	Michael Gouby '1860T' (see bibliography) Fine: £200				
	ND	E over P in PENNY. Fine: £950. Only 1 known.				

1861 Mintage: 36,449,280

D	18	Signature	£60	£180	£500	
F	20	No signature	£30	£150	£400	
D	21	LCW almost touches border, see Freeman. EF: £5500				
D	22	Signature below	£7	£20	£80	£200/£260
G	25	No signature	£140			
D	26	No signature, 15 leaves	£15	£75	£200	
D	29	No signature, 16 leaves	£10	£40	£100	£250/
G	33	6 over 8	£700			
G	33	No signature	£7	£25	£80	£150/

Above is the obverse type with 15 leaves (and 4 berries). When counting, use a good lens and don't forget the leaves below the strands of hair which are swept over the ear!

Reverse C. Very similar to Reverse A but with small rock to left of the lighthouse.

VICTORIA Bun Head, date below Britannia, Bronze 30.81mm (continued)

Date	FMAN	Mintage	Fine	VF	EF	UNC/BU
1862	38	With signature (refer to Freeman, see bibliography)				£4000/
1862	ND	2 of date over 1	Near Fine: £1050			
1862	39	50,534,400	£2	£9	£40	£120/
1862	41	Date from halfpenny die (smaller): Good Fine: £1600 (Bamford 2006)				
1862	39A	8 over 6			£1500	£2000/
1863	42	28,062,720	£2	£12	£65	£150/£200
1863	45	'2' below date			£4000 (Bamford 2006)	
1863	46	'3' below date			£2400 (Bamford 2006)	
1863	47	'4' below date	Good: £2000 (Bamford 2006)			
1863	ND	'5' below date, only one known. Very very worn: £18,000				
1863	ND	'3' with shorter lower serif in date. £1350 (Bamford 2006)				
[See book: 'The British Bronze Penny'. More details in bibliography section.]						
1864*	49	3,440,646, Type A	£40	£100	£450	£900
1864*	48	Inc above. Type B			£1250 (Bamford 2006)	
1865	50	8,601,600	£7	£30	£60	£250/£350
1865	51	5 over 3	£40	£150	£600	£1100/
1866	52	9,999,360	£15	£30	£75	£200/
1867	53	5,483,520	£12	£70	£250	£460/
1868	56	1,182,720	£12	£70	£250	£460/
1869	59	2,580,480	£85	£350	£1500	£2300/
1870	60	5,695,022	£7	£30	£90	£340/
1870	ND	Narrower date			£250	
1871	61	1,290,318	£100	£200	£400	£800/
1872	62	8,494,572	£7	£25	£100	£210/
1873	63	8,494,200	£7	£25	£70	£180/
1874		4 varieties. Freeman 65, 67, 70 and 72. Valuations similar.				
		5,621,865	£12	£50	£160	£380/£450
1874H		4 varieties. Freeman 66, 68, 71 and 73.				
		6,666,240	Fine: £12-£30 VF:£50-£100 EF:£150-£300			
1875	80	10,691,040	£10	£60	£350	£840/
1875	82	Wider date, thicker trident			£60	£350/
1875H	85	752,640	£40	£400	£700	£1500/
1876H	87	11,074,560	£8	£30	£200	£350/
1876H	89	Narrow date			£80	£200/
1876H	ND	With missing 'H'	Fair: £230 (Bamford 2006)			
1877	90	Small, narrow date. Fair: £3100 (Bamford 2006)				
1877	91	9,624,747	£6	£20	£100	£150/
1878	94	2,764,470	£8	£25	£100	£250/£400
1879*	96	7,666,476. Type A	£20	£100	£300	
1879*	97	Inc above. Type B	£4	£15	£100	£200/
1879	98	Small date	£70		£500	
1880*	99	3,000,831	£5	£20	£140	£350/
1881	102	2,302,261	£4	£18	£130	£350/
1881*	106	Portrait 'aged' further			£450	
1881H	108	3,763,200	£4	£20	£150	£280/£500
1882H	111	7,526,400	£4	£16	£130	£300/
1882H	ND	2 over 1			£350	
1882	112	No H*	£820 (Bamford 2006)			

* 1864 types A and B concern the '4' in the date. Type A '4's have an upper pointing serif coming off the right side of the horizontal crossbar of the '4'. Type B '4's have a 'T' shaped end on the horizontal part of the '4'.

*1879 Type A/B pennies have minor obverse differences. One of the easiest to spot (on higher grade coins) is that Type B has double incuse lines for leaf veins, whereas Type A has just a single line.

*1880 Pennies either have rocks to the left of the lighthouse, or not. The image above shows rocks. Values are the same.

*The aged portrait of 1881 is difficult to spot with worn coins, the easiest method is to count the leaves in the wreath - the aged portrait has 15, the normal version has 17.

*There are two 1883 varieties (FMAN 116 and 118) but most dealers do not distinguish. The easiest way to tell the difference is one has the 'RI' of BRITT joined at the bottom, the other doesn't.

• Beware of 1882H coins so worn that the 'H' is worn away, and of coins that have had the 'H' deliberately removed.

VICTORIA Bun Head, date below Britannia, Bronze 30.8lmm (continued)

Date	FMAN	Mintage	Fine	VF	EF	UNC/BU
1883*	116/8	6,237,438	£6	£15	£40	£110/
1884	119	11,702,802	£3	£10	£40	£110/£150
1885	121	7,145,862	£3	£10	£40	£110/
1886	123	6,087,759	£3	£10	£40	£110/
1887	125	5,315,085	£4	£15	£60	£130/
1888	126	5,125,020	£5	£20	£45	£120/£210
1889	127	12,559,737 15 leaves	£5	£15	£45	£120/
1889	128	Narrow date 14 leaves in wreath		£75	£180/
1890	130	15,330,840	£3	£12	£40	£100/£150
1890	ND	Narrow date		£200		
1891	132	17,885,961	£2	£10	£30	£70/
1891	ND	Wide spaced date				£340/
1892	134	10,501,671	£2	£10	£40	£100/
1892	ND	Narrow spaced date. Fair: £15				
1893	136	8,161,737	£2	£10	£40	£110/
1894	138	3,883,452	£6	£20	£50	£150/£220

Dies were engraved by George William de Saulles for the veiled head final victoria issue. The obverse was copied from a model by Thomas Brock, and the reverse was a modified version of the Leonard Charles Wyon type.

VICTORIA Old or Widow Head, Bronze 30.8lmm. Weight 9.467g

Date	FMAN	Mintage	Fine	VF	EF	UNC/BU
1895	141	5,395,830 Rev B		£5	£25	£80/
1895*	139	Rev A	£30	£150	£500	
1896	143	24,147,156	£1	£5	£15	£35/£55
1897	145	20,756,620	£1	£3	£8	£25/£35
1897	147	Spot between O and N in ONE				£1000/
1897*	148	Higher tide			£200	£500/£600
1898	149	14,296,836	£1	£3	£14	£40/£60
1899	150	26,441,069	£1	£4	£15	£40/£50
1900	153	31,778,109		£2	£10	£20/£50
1901	154	22,205,568	£1	£8		£20/£35
1901	ND	With milled edge Fair: £42 [London Coins 2007]				

1895 - Rev A: trident to the 'P' is 2mm. No sea behind Britannia and to the right of Britannia the tide is very low (see image above).

Rev B: trident to P is 1mm. Sea present behind (to left of) Britannia and the tide level to the right is higher.

1897 - Right: The higher tide meets Britannia well above the hemline. The normal tide coin is illustrated.

Victoria Penny 1901

Right: Many Veiled head pennies have wider spaced dates. Sometimes a premium for extra-wide or very narrow spacing can be added to the value.

The dies for this issue were also by George William de Saulles ('De S' can be seen beneath the bust). Pennie struck early in 1902 used the same reverse as the veiled head Victoria issue. This die was slightly change during 1902, resulting in the low tide, and normal tide types.

EDWARD VII Bronze 30.8lmm. Weight 9.435g

Date	FMAN	Mintage	Fine	VF	EF	UNC/BU
1902	156	Low tide	£6	£20	£65	£100/£150
		Minor date pointing varieties occur for the above.				
1902	157	26,976,768	50p	£3	£5	£15/£35
1903	158	21,415,296		£4	£10	£40/£55
1903	158A	Open '3' (bottom serif points at the '0')				
				£100 (not seen better than GF)		
1904	159	12,913,152		£5	£25	£70/£120
1905*	160/1	17,783,808		£4	£20	£55/
1906	162	37,989,504		£4	£12	£40/
1907	163	47,322,240		£3	£12	£40/
1908*	164-6	31,506,048		£3	£10	£45/
1909	168	19,617,024 '1' right of tooth			£9	£40/£65
1909	169	'1' is directly above tooth			£35	£70/£100
1910	170	29,549,184		£4	£20	£40/

*1905 FMAN 160 and 161 either have upright part of the 'E' in 'PENNY' pointing at a rim bead or at a gap.

*1908 FMAN 164,164A,165 and 166 - Four slight varieties, most are common with the exception of 164A which has the colon after BRITT pointing to a rim tooth. This variety is rare.

Edward Penny 1902

The image above shows the 1902 low tide type; the tide is about level with the hemline. The image below shows the 1902 penny normal tide, which is higher and roughly level with where the legs cross.

George V 1912 H Penny.
Large (first) head obverse.

The BM initials on the truncation of George V stand for Bertram Mackennal, the designer of the George V bust. The first reverse type was identical to that used for Edward VII. There were big problems with 'ghosting' (see also George V Half penny notes) for this issue throughout most of the reign. Despite the head being modified in 1926 and some changes to the reverse, this problem was not completely solved until the issue of the smaller head type in 1928. The 1912, 1918 and 1919 H/KN pennies have the mintmark to the left of the date. Some 1912H pennies are 1/10 mm greater in diameter.

GEORGE V Bronze 30.8Imm . Weight 9.45g

Date	FMAN	Mintage	Fine	VF	EF	UNC/BU
1911	171	23,079,168		£4	£8	£30/£40
1912	172	48,306,048		£3	£12	£30/
1912H	173	16,800,000		£12	£70	£150/
1913*	174-7	65,497,872		£5	£35	£60/
1914	178	50,820,997		£3	£15	£40/
1915	179	47,310,807		£3	£15	£40/
1915 and 1916 with ear recessed, add approx 20%						
1916	180	86,411,165		£2	£15	£40/
1917	181	107,905,436		£2	£8	£25/£40
1918	182	84,227,372		£2	£8	£25/£40
1918H	183	3,660,800	£3	£25	£150	£300/
1918KN	184		£10	£100	£400	£600/
1919	185	113,761,090		£1	£10	£35/
1919H	186	5,209,600	£3	£100	£300	£500/
1919KN	187	Inc above	£10	£70	£300	£1000/
1920	188	124,693,485		£2	£8	£30/
1920	189	Colon after IMP points at a tooth. Ext. rare.				
1921*	190/1	129,717,693		£2	£10	£30/£35
1922	192	16,346,711		£3	£18	£30/£50
1922	192A	Centre trident prong well below tooth. Fine: £1200 (2006)				
1926	193	4,498,519		£20	£80	£110/
1926	195	Modified effigy, see app 1	£40	£100	£500	£2000/
1927	197	60,989,561		£2	£15	£25/
1928	199	50,178.000		£2	£15	£25/
1929	201	49,132,800		£1	£15	£25/
1930	203	29,097,600		£1	£10	£20/£40
1931	205	19,843,200		£1	£10	£25/£35
1932	207	8,277,600		£3	£15	£35/£45
1933*		7 or 8+ 'patterns'	£45,000 (2006)			
1933*		Pattern by Lavrillier £4,100 (1986)				
1933*		A uniface £28,750 (1980)	£40,000+ (estimated)			
1933*		Modern reproduction 'patterns' are plentiful. £20/£25				
1934	210	13,965,600		£2	£10	£30/£40
1935	212	56,070,000		£1	£3	£8/£20
1936	214	154,296,000		£1	£2	£4/£10

*1913 - Four minor varieties, all are fairly common and distinguishing them depends on the pointing of the 'P' on the reverse, and the position of the colon between 'GRA : BRITT'.

*1921 FMAN 190 and 191 - Two varieties occur, they can be differentiated by looking at the colon after 'DEF'. The 190 colon points to a gap, the 191 colon points to a tooth. Values are about the same.

*1933 Pennies shouldn't really be listed in the circulated coins area because none were struck for circulation. I thought I'd keep it here for completeness as it is one of those legendary British coins.

George V 1935 Penny

George V 1933 Pattern Penny. Struck at the Royal Mint with dies by Frenchman André Lavrillier. It is thought there are only 4 in existance. The one shown here is from the British Museum collection.

EDWARD VIII Bronze 30.8Imm

Date	FMAN	Mintage	VF	EF	UNC/BU
1937		Specimen strikings only, from			£35,000

Edward VIII Penny from the British
Museum Collection.

GEORGE VI Bronze 30.8Imm. Weight 9.442g

The obverse was engraved from a model by Thomas Humphrey Paget and the reverse was a slightly different Britannia type, modified by Royal Mint staff. During the war tin became scarce, so the percentage in the bronze alloy was reduced from 3% to 0.5%. The coins dated 1944 - 46 were also chemically darkened to give them the same tones as the previous un-treated coins. With all George VI coins, the titles IND:IMP were removed in 1949.

Date	FMAN	Mintage	Fine	VF	EF	UNC/BU
1937*	217/9	88,896,000			£1	£3/£8
1937*	218/20	26,402 Proofs			£3	£4/£8
1938	222	121,560,000			£1	£10/£15
1939	224	55,560,000			£2	£15/£25
1940	226	42,284,400		£3	£7	£30/£35
1940*	227	Double exergue line			£5	£10/£20
1944*	229	42,600,000		60p	£3	£6/£9
1944*	ND	Not darkened by Mint				£10/£25
1945	231	79,531,200		£1	£5	£18/
1945	ND	Doubled 9		£5	£25	
1946	233	66,355,600			£2	£8/£10
1947	235	2,220,400			£1	£4/£6
1948	236	63,961,200			£1	£3/£4
1949	238	14,324,400			£1	£4/£6
1950	240	240,000		£8	£18	£25/£35
1950	241	17,513 Proofs			FDC	£30
1951	242	120,000	£3	£8	£12	£30/£40
1951	243	20,000 Proofs			FDC	£35
1952		(2006 Rasmussen)				£37,500

*1937 FMAN 217 and 219 - Two varieties occur with alternate pointings for the 2nd upright of the 'N' in 'ONE'. Both are fairly common and the same varieties are also found in the proof 1937 Pennies, FMAN 218 and 220.

*1940 FMAN 227. Below is an example of the double exergue 1940 penny

*1944 FMAN 229 - Unconfirmed sightings of a 1944 penny with the waves reaching slightly into the exergue.

George VI Penny first obverse
with IND IMP.

George VI 1951 Penny

ELIZABETH II Bronze 30.81mm. Weight 9.396g

Date	FMAN	Mintage	VF	EF	UNC/BU
1953*	245	1,308,400		£3	£8/£12
1953	246	40,000 Proofs			£10/£18
1954		1 retrieved from change. Now in British Museum.			
1954		Another (2006 Rasmussen) £37,500			
1961	248	48,313,400			£2/£3
1962	250	157,588,600			£2/£3
1963	252	119,733,600			£2/£3
1964	254	153,294,000			£1/£2
1965	255	121,310,400			£1/£2
1966	256	165,739,200			/£1
1967	257	654,564,000**			/50p
1970	257A	750,424 Proofs from the set			£4/£5

* 1953 non proof pennies were only issued originally in the 9 coin plastic sets.
** 1967 Mintage includes pennies minted in 1968, 69 and 70 but dated 1967.

Elizabeth II 1964 Penny

Three Halfpences or One and a Half pence

These tiny coins were issued for use in some colonies, and were never legal tender in the UK. They are included here because, like the fractional farthings, they are at the very least relatives of the normal British Coinage, and they do bear the latin word 'Brittanniar' (Britain). I wonder how many of these tiddlers ended up down the back of sofas, never again to see the light of day.

WILLIAM IV .925 fine Silver 12mm. Weight 0.7g

Date	FMAN	Mintage	Fine	VF	EF	UNC/BU
1834	2250	800,448	£6	£15	£35	£80/
1835	2251	633,600	£10	£20	£55	£110/
1835	2251A	5 over 4	£6	£15	£40	£80/
1836	2252	158,400	£5	£15	£30	£70/
1837	2253	30,624	£10	£40	£100	£180/

William IV 1834 Threehalfpence

VICTORIA .925 fine Silver 12mm. Weight 0.7g

Date	FMAN	Mintage	Fine	VF	EF	UNC/BU
1838	2254	538,560	£6	£10	£30	£65/
1839	2255	760,320	£4	£10	£30	£65/
1840	2256	95,040	£8	£20	£70	£120/
1841	2257	158,400	£6	£15	£40	£90/
1842	2258	1,869,120	£4	£10	£30	£80/
1843	2259	475,200	£4	£12	£28	£60/
1843	2259B	43/34	£10	£30	£100	£180/
1860	2260	160,000	£5	£20	£35	£65/£95
1862	2261	256,000	£5	£20	£60	£100/

Victoria 1839 Threehalfpence

Cartwheel Twopence

The heaviest British coin ever circulated, Cartwheel twopences are 41mm in diameter, over 5mm thick, and weigh almost 60 grammes each. With the Cartwheel Penny (see penny section) these two coins were the first to be struck for circulation by the new steam powered presses installed by James Watt at the premises of Matthew Boulton in Soho, Birmingham. Those two men changed the shape (quite literally!) of British coinage and set the standard for all coins that followed. The fact they are such heavy coins means they are more likely to show signs of edge damage. Serious, or multiple edge knocks will result in lower values.

GEORGE III Copper 41mm. Weight 2oz/56.7g (official)

Date	Peck	Mintage	Fine	VF	EF	UNC/BU
1797	P1077	722,160	£20	£45	£110	£300/

George III Cartwheel Twopence

£15.50 Each

price shown is per tray.

PULAR LINDNER
IN BOXES

...ost popular storage solution for coins. Coin ...s are available in a wide range of formats to ...oins from 16.5mm up to 63mm. With round ...are inserts. Most coin boxes are designed ... stackable, making them ideal for storing on ...lf, or even in a safe. All the coin boxes we ...selected are made from acid free materials ...id damage to your coins.

...tock Lindner coin boxes in 132 ...ent combinations. Please call us for ...test brochure.

Round Compartment for 29.5mm coins
Round Compartment for 39mm coins
Square Compartment for 24mm coins
Square Compartment for 30mm coins
Square Compartment for 36mm coins
Square Compartment for assorted sizes

Box: 2145

Box: 2580

Box: 2535

KARAT ALBUM
Album with 10 assorted pages and interleaving
£24.20
with slipcase
£32.30

8015 LINDNER Coin Cleaner, for all metals 250 ml
£9.25

LINDNER Precious Metal Dip
8010 for gold and silver coins, 375 ml **£10.25**
8011 for copper, nickel and brass coins 375 ml **£10.25**

SILBO CLEANING BATHS FOR COINS
8012 for silver coins
£8.30
8013 for copper and brass coins **£8.30**
8014 gold bath for all types of gold, as well as patinated and goldplated pieces.
£6.45

CALL TODAY FOR A FREE BROCHURE!

2014 LINDNER Coin Tongs, Protective ends for safe handling of yo... coins. **£2.65**

LINDNER COIN CAPSULES
The best protection for your coins! Price per 10.

Size	Example Coin	Suitable Box	Price
18.0mm	Dec' Half Penny	2505/2905	£3.25
20.0mm	Half Sovereign	2550/2950	£3.25
21.0mm	Farthing 1860+	2510/2910	£3.25
21.5mm	Twenty Pence	2510/2910	£3.25
22.0mm	Farthing 1821	2580/2980	£3.25
23.0mm	One Pound	2108/2708	£3.25
23.5mm	Farthing 1799	2108/2708	£3.25
24.0mm	Shilling	2549/2949	£3.25
26.0mm	Half Penny	2109/2709	£3.25
28.0mm	Half Penny 1825	2105/2705	£3.25
29.0mm	Two Pound	2105/2705	£3.25
30.0mm	Fifty Pence	2125/2725	£3.25
31.0mm	Penny 1860-1967	2104/2704	£3.25
32.5mm	Half Crown	2130/2730	£3.25
34.0mm	Penny 1825-1860	2150/2750	£3.25
35.0mm	Penny 1806-07	2101/2701	£3.70
36.0mm	Double Florin	2101/2701	£3.70
39.0mm	Crown	2106/2706	£3.70

COIN CARRY CASE & TRAYS
Aluminium design case with 6 coin trays.

1x tray for 24mm coins
4x tray for 34mm coins
1x tray for 47mm coins
£32.10

Extra trays: **£2.70 Each**

EL. 01736 751910   WWW.PRINZ.CO.UK
PRINZ PUBLICATIONS UK LTD, UNIT 3A HAYLE INDUSTRIAL PARK, HAYLE, CORNWALL, TR27 5JR
UK POSTAGE: ORDERS UP TO £50 POSTAGE £2.50. ORDERS OVER £50 POST FREE. OVERSEAS POSTAGE CHARGED AT COST

Threepences

Later George III, all George IV and early William IV Threepences:
At some point in the late 1700s/early 1800s (the jury is still out on exactly when) the threepence stopped being a circulating coin minted in large numbers, and was only minted for use in the annual Maundy ceremony. The circulation of a currency threepence for use in the United Kingdon was re-started in the early part of Queen Victoria's reign. For this reason, the threepences dated between 1800 - 1833 can be found in the Maundy section.

WILLIAM IV .925 fine Silver 16mm. Weight 1.414g

All the non-Maundy William IV threepences listed here were only issued for use in the West Indies. They do not have a prooflike mirror finish like the Maundy threepences.

Date	ESC	Details	Fine	VF	EF	UNC/BU
1831-1833 - Maundy type only see Maundy section.						
1834	2044	401,016	£5	£20	£45	£150/
1835	2045	491,040	£5	£20	£60	£160/
1836	2046	411,840	£5	£20	£60	£160/
1837	2047	42,768	£10	£25	£60	£160/

VICTORIA .925 fine Silver 16mm.. Weight 1.414g

Young Head, as Maundy type but without prooflike mirrored surface. The bust was changed slightly in 1859, 1867 and 1880, although some later coins were struck using earlier dies. A comprehensive listing of the four obverse types and two different reverses is given in 'English Silver Coins' by P Alan Rayner.

Date	ESC	Details	Fine	VF	EF	UNC/BU
1838*	2048	1,203,840	£6	£18	£60	£150/
1838*	2048A	BRITANNIAB error			Extremely rare	
1839*	2049	570,240	£8	£20	£65	£150/£175
1840*	2050	633,600	£7	£20	£65	£150/
1841*	2051	443,520	£7	£28	£70	£180/
1842*	2052	2,027,520	£8	£15	£60	£150/
1843*	2053	Inc above	£7	£15	£60	£150/
1844*	2054	1,045,400	£5	£15	£65	£130/
1845	2055	1,314,720	£8	£20	£60	£120/
1846	2056	47,520	£15	£40	£120	£250/
1847*	ND	Unknown			£375	
1848*	2056A	Unknown	£50	£150	£350	
1849	2057	126,720	£7	£18	£65	£110/
1850	2058	950,400	£6	£15	£50	£125/
1851	2059	479,065	£7	£15	£55	£120/
1851	2059A	5/8	£12	£30	£80	£180/£200
1852	2059B		£60	£200	£450	£950/
1853	2060	31,680	£20	£40	£140	£250/
1854	2061	1,467,246	£7	£18	£60	£150/
1855	2062	383,350	£8	£25	£80	£175/
1856	2063	1,013,760	£8	£25	£80	£175/
1857	2064	1,758,240	£8	£25	£80	£175/
1858	2065	1,441,440	£6	£10	£50	£100/
1858	2065A	BRITANNIAB	£30	£120	£250	
1859	2066	3,579,840	£7	£15	£50	£110/
1860	2067	3,405,600	£7	£15	£50	£110/
1861	2068	3,294,720	£7	£15	£60	£120/
1862	2069	1,156,320	£8	£15	£60	£120/
1863	2070	950,400	£7	£15	£60	£120/
1864	2071	1,330,560	£7	£15	£50	£110/
1865	2072	1,742,400	£7	£15	£60	£120/

*Issued for colonial use only

Victoria Threepence 1864

VICTORIA .925 fine Silver 16mm.. Weight 1.414g [continued]

Date	ESC	Details	Fine	VF	EF	UNC/BU
1866	2073	1,900,800	£7	£15	£50	£110/
1866	2073	1,900,800	£7	£15	£50	£110/
1867	2074	712,800	£7	£15	£50	£110/
1868	2075	1,457,280	£7	£15	£50	£110/
1868	2075A	RRITANNIAR	£40	£100		
1869	2075C	4,488 Maundy	£8	£16	£65	£95/£135
1870	2076	1,283,218	£5	£10	£45	£70/£100
1871	2077	999,633	£5	£10	£45	£70/£100
1872	2078	1,293,271	£7	£15	£50	£110/
1873	2079	4,055,550	£5	£12	£28	£80/£100
1874	2080	4,427,031	£5	£12	£30	£65/£80
1875	2081	3,306,500	£5	£8	£28	£65/£80
1876	2082	1,834,389	£5	£10	£30	£65/
1877	2083	2,622,393	£5	£10	£38	£70/
1878	2084	2,419,975	£10	£20	£40	£85/
1879	2085	3,140,265	£9	£15	£45	£85/
1880	2087	1,610,069	£6	£10	£30	£65/
1881	2088	3,248,265	£4	£9	£28	£55/
1882	2089	472,965	£10	£30	£70	£120/
1883	2090	4,365,971	£4	£8	£25	£60/£80
1884	2091	3,322,424	£5	£10	£35	£65/
1885	2092	5,183,653	£4	£10	£25	£50/£60
1886	2093	6,152,669	£4	£9	£28	£50/£60
1887	2094	2,780,761	£4	£10	£30	£75/

Victoria Young Head 1878 Threepence

The controversial Jubilee head bust (some people have remarked that it made the Queen look like a penguin, with a ridiculously small crown) was designed by Joseph Edgar Boehm.

VICTORIA .925 fine Silver 16mm Jubilee head (JH). Weight 1.414g

Date	ESC	Details	Fine	VF	EF	UNC/BU
1887	2096	Inc above	£2	£4	£6	£15/£20
1887	2097	Proof				/£95
1888	2098	518,199	£5	£10	£28	£45/
1889	2099	4,587,010	£2	£4	£10	£30/
1890	2100	4,465,834	£2	£4	£10	£30/
1891	2101	6,323,027	£2	£4	£10	£30/
1892	2102	2,578,226	£2	£5	£10	£30/
1893	2103	3,067,243	£14	£35	£100	£250/

Victoria Jubilee Head 1887 Threepence

Dies were engraved by George William de Saulles for the veiled head final victoria issue. The obverse was copied from a model by Thomas Brock.

VICTORIA .925 fine Silver 16mm Old, or Widow head. Weight 1.414g

Date	ESC	Details	Fine	VF	EF	UNC/BU
1893	2104	Inc with JH	£2	£5	£10	£20/£25
1893	2105	1,312 Proofs				/£90
1894	2106	1,608,603	£3	£5	£18	£36/
1895	2107	4,788,609	£3	£5	£12	£22/
1896	2108	4,598,442	£3	£5	£12	£22/
1897	2109	4,541,294	£2	£4	£12	£22/
1898	2110	4,567,177	£2	£4	£12	£22/
1899	2111	6,246,281	£2	£4	£12	£22/
1900	2112	10,644,480	£2	£3	£10	£20/
1901	2113	6,098,400	£1	£4	£8	£22/

Victoria Veiled Head 1898 Threepence

EDWARD VII .925 fine Silver 16mm. Weight 1.414g

George William de Saulles engraved the Edward VII bust.

Date	ESC	Mintage	Fine	VF	EF	UNC/BU
1902	2114	8,268,480	£1	£2	£5	£15/£20
1902	2115	15,123 Proofs				£15/£20
1903	2116	5,227,200	£3	£8	£22	£40/£50
1904	2117	3,627,360	£6	£9	£35	£50/
1905	2118	3,548,160	£7	£11	£50	
1906	2119	3,152,160	£3	£8	£20	£40/£45
1907	2120	4,831,200	£2	£5	£10	£25/£30
1908	2121	8,157,600	£2	£5	£12	£25/£35
1909	2122	4,055,040	£2	£8	£20	£40/
1910	2123	4,563,380	£1	£4	£12	£30/

Edward VII Threepence obverse.
Reverse type was as the early
Geroge V Threepence (below)

GEORGE V .925 fine Silver 16mm. Weight 1.414g

The bust was by Bertram MacKennal, the reverse was carried over from the previous type until the acorn type was adopted in 1927, and ran to the end of the reign.

Date	ESC	Mintage	Fine	VF	EF	UNC/BU
1911	2124	5,841,084	90p	£2	£7	£18/£25
1911	2125	6,001 Proofs				£20/
1912	2126	8,932,825	70p	£3	£9	£15/£20
1913	2127	7,143,242	£1	£4	£7	£20/£30
1914	2128	6,733,584	70p	£2	£6	£20/£25
1915	2129	5,450,617	70p	£2	£6	£20/£25
1916	2130	18,555,201	70p	£1	£4	£20/£25
1917	2131	21,662,490	70p	£1	£4	£20/£25
1918	2132	20,630,909	70p	£1	£4	£20/£25
1919	2133	16,845,687	70p	£1	£4	£20/£25
1920*	2134	16,703,597		£2	£6	£25/
Now debased .500 (50%) silver, type and size as previous.						
1920*	2135	.500 silver		£1	£5	£20/
1921	2136	8,749,301	£1	£3	£9	£25
1922	2137	7,979,998	£1	£2	£8	£20/£25
1925	2138	3,731,859	£1	£5	£10	£30/£40
1926	2139	4,107,910	£1	£4	£10	£25/£30
1926	2140	Modified Effigy (Ap 1)		£4	£8	£20/£30
1927	2141	15,022 Proofs			£50	£70/£90
1928	2142	1,302,106	£1	£4	£12	£28/£35
1930	2143	1,319,412	£2	£5	£15	£28/£35
1931	2144	6,251,936		£1	£5	£10/£14
1932	2145	5,887,325		£1	£5	£10/£14
1933	2146	5,578,541		£1	£3	£10/£12
1934	2147	7,405,954		£1	£2	£8/£10
1935	2148	7,027,654		£1	£2	£7/£9
1936	2149	3,238,670		£1	£2	£7/£9

George V Threepence 1920

* Sterling silver 1920 threepences have slightly stronger details, particularly on the serifs of the 'E's, owing to a slight difference in the resistance of the different alloys. Very difficult to spot, and good magnification is needed. Many dealers don't bother, as both are worth about the same.

George V Threepence,
2nd Reverse type (1927-1936)

EDWARD VIII

Date	ESC	Mintage	Fine	VF	EF	UNC/BU
1937	2149D	Pattern, 3 rings on reverse. At least			£9500/£12000	

GEORGE VI .500 fine Silver 16mm. Weight 1.414g

New reverses were used for nearly all the George VI denominations. The silver threepence featured a St George's cross on a Tudor rose and was designed by George Kruger Gray, whose initials can be seen on many of the George VI reverses. The portrait was by Thomas Humphrey Paget.

Date	ESC	Mintage	Fine	VF	EF	UNC/BU
1937	2150	8,148,156		50p	£2	£6/£7
1937	2151	26,402 Proofs				£8/£10
1938	2152	6,402,473		50p	£3	£10/£12
1939	2153	1,355,860		50p	£4	£14/
1940	2154	7,914,401		50p	£3	£12/
1941	2155	7,979,411		50p	£4	£16/
1942*	2156	4,144,051	£1	£6	£14	£35/
1943*	2157	1,379,220	£2	£5	£15	£38/
1944*	2158	2,005,553	£3	£10	£30	£50/
1945	2159	371,000	(1997: VF £4000)			

George VI Silver 1943 Threepence

Most 1945 coins were melted down.
*For Colonial use only.

Threepences dodecagonal (12 sided) nickel-brass

EDWARD VIII

Officially, no coins bearing the portrait of Edward VIII were issued for circulation despite the fact that all the dies were prepared for all the denominations, and proofs were struck for approval. However, the brass threepence, being a new size and type was produced in slightly higher numbers, primarily for testing in vending machines. A handful of these coins were sent to vending machine manufacturers, and not all were returned! The obverse portrait was by Thomas Humprey Paget and the reverse Thrift plant by Madge Kitchener. Normal thickness, and thinner varieties of this extremely rare coin are known to exist.

Date	Peck		UNC/BU
1937	2365/6	Date divided by THRIFT PLANT (Sea-pink); thicknesses vary. Cooke (1994)	£24,500
1937	2366	As George VI type but effigy of Edward VIII. Coincraft (1999)	£20,000

A current estimate would perhaps be £35,000+ for any type Edward VIII threepence.

Edward VIII Brass 1937 Threepence

GEORGE VI Nickel-brass, 12 sided, 21mm. 6.8g

A modified version of the intended Edward VIII reverse was used for the brass threepences of George VI. At first they were issued simultaneously with the usual small silver type of threepence. Within a few years the silver type was phased out and the twelve sided (dodecagonal) thick brass threepence was struck until 1967 (and in 1970 for the proof set). Early on, the Royal Mint found that the twelve sided collar placed around each coin before striking was prone to weaknesses, especially in the twelve sharp corners. During WWII the quantity of steel available for making these collars declined so in order to make the collars last longer, they were re-made with blunter corners. This experimentation led to a couple of the dates being struck with either sharp or rounded corners. See box below for more details.

Date	Peck	Mintage	Fine	VF	EF	UNC/BU
1937*	2370	45,707,957		50p	£1	£3/£5
1937	2371	26,402 Proofs			£3	£9/£15
1938	2372	14,532,332		50p	£5	£22/£28
1939	2374	5,603,021		£1	£4	£30/£35
1940	2376	12,636,018		£2	£6	£20/£25
1941**	2378/2379A	60,239,489		£1	£2	£9/£10
1942	2380	103,214,400		£1	£2	£9/£10
1943	2382	101,702,400		£1	£2	£9/£10
1944	2384	69,760,000		£1	£2	£10/£12
1945	2386	33,942,466		£1	£3	£14/£20
1946	2388	620,734	£10	£60	£200	
1948**	2390/1	4,230,400		£2	£8	£35/£50
1949	2392	464,000	£6	£50	£150	
1950	2394	1,600,000		£3	£15	£30/£50
1950	2395	17,513 Proofs				£15/£25
1951	2396	1,184,000		£5	£18	£40/£60
1951	2397	20,000 Proofs				£30/£40
1952	2398	25,494,400			£1	£12/£16

George VI Brass 1937 Threepence

*1937 - Two different spacings from rim to word THREE noted. They are not normally distinguished between.

**Sharp and rounded corners: Varieties of George VI threepences exist with either sharp or rounded corners.

1937 - 1940: All Sharp
1941: Sharp or Rounded.
1942 - 1946: All Rounded
1948: Sharp or Rounded
1949: All Rounded
1950 - 1952: All Sharp

ELIZABETH II Nickel-brass, 12 sided. Size/Weight as GVI

William Gardner designed the new porcullis reverse for the brass threepences of Elizabeth II. Mary Gillick was responsible for the young (first) Elizabeth II effigy.

Date	Peck	Mintage	EF	UNC/BU
1953*	2489	30,618,000. Obv 1		£2/£4
1953*	2490	Inc above. Obv 2	£2	£4/£6
1953*	2491	40,000 Proofs		£4/£6
1954	2492	41,720,000	£1	£6/£7
1955	2494	41,075,200	£1	£6/£7
1956	2496	36,801,600	£2	£7/£8
1957	2498	24,294,400	£2	£6/£7
1958	2500	20,504,000	£2	£8/£10
1959	2501A	28,499,200	£1	£5/£6
1960	2501C	83,078,400		£2/£4
1961	2501E	41,102,400		£2/£3
1962	2501G	51,545,600		£1/£2
1963	2501I	35,280,000		£1/£2
1964	ND**	44,867,200		£1/£2
1965	ND**	27,160,000		£1/£2
1966	ND**	53,760,000		60p/£1
1967	ND**	151,780,800		50p/£1
1970	ND**	750,476 Proofs from set		£3/£4
Undated error - double obverse				£375

Elizabeth II Brass 1960 Threepence

*1953 Threepences have 2 distict levels of definition to the Queen's head. The poorly defined Obv 1 type is ex the 1953 specimen set. The sharper Obv 2 is the normal issue, a similar sharper die was also used for the 1953 proofs.

*1953 - Varieties exist with either the I of ELIZABETH pointing to a corner or with it pointing much further to the right.

** The Peck reference work was compiled in 1963. No coins newer than 1963 were catalogued.

Fourpences (Groats), non Maundy 'Britannia' type

WILLIAM IV Britannia on reverse .925 fine Silver, 16mm. Weight 1.89g

The William IV Britannia type groats were issued for use in British Guiana to replace the Quarter Guilder. The design and wording is the same as later British issues, and for that reason these coins are included here. Unlike the silver threepence, which is the same size, the Britannia groats have a milled edge.

Date	ESC	Mintage	Fine	VF	EF	UNC/BU
1836	1918	4,253,000	£5	£18	£35	£85/£140
1836	ND	Colons close to D	£5	£25	£70	
1837	1922	962,280	£9	£15	£40	£95/£140

VICTORIA Britannia on reverse .925 fine Silver, 16mm. Weight 1.87g

The reverse used for the Young head Victorian Britannia groats was the same as that used previously for William IV. The effigy is that designed by William Wyon.

William IV 1836 Groat

Date	ESC	Mintage	Fine	VF	EF	UNC/BU
1838	1930	2,150,280	£6	£10	£32	£75/£85
1838	1931A	2nd 8 struck over sideways 8	£10	£20	£40	£100/£150
1839	1932	1,461,240	£5	£10	£40	£65/£100
1840	1934	1,496,880	£6	£15	£40	£80/£90
1840	1934A	Zero in date rounder, like letter O				
1840	ND	0 (zero) struck over rounder O. Reported 1994.				
1841	1935	344,520	£6	£12	£40	£80/£90
1841	ND	2nd 1 over upside-down 1		£60	£100	
1842	1936	724,680	£6	£12	£45	£90/£100
1842	1937A	2 struck over 1	£8	£15	£80	
1843	1938	1,817,640	£6	£12	£45	£70/£90
1843	1938A	4 over 5	£8	£20	£50	£90/£100
1843	ND.	Double 4 in date	£8	£20	(reported 2005)	
1844	1939	855,360	£6	£12	£60	£110/£140
1845	1940	914,760	£4	£6	£40	£100/
1846	1941	1,366,200	£4	£15	£45	£75/£100
1847	1942	226,000 7 over 6	£15	£60	£240	
1848	1943	712,800	£5	£10	£45	£70/£85
1848	1944	2nd 8 over 6	£20	£50	£200	£450/
1848	1944A	2nd 8 over 7	£6	£15	£45	£85/£95
1849	1945	380,160	£6	£12	£45	£70/£90
1849	1946	9 over 8	£5	£10	£50	£70/£90
1851	1947	594,000	£30	£100	£300	£600/
1852	1948	31,300	£50	£200	£550	
1853	1949	11,880	£30	£120	£300	£600/
1854	1952	1,096,613	£4	£10	£40	£70/£90
1854	ND	5 struck over 3	£3	£15	£50	£100/£120
1855	1953	646,041	£5	£10	£40	£85/£100

Victoria 1848 Groat.
The Jubilee Head Groats had the same reverse with the standard Jubilee Head obverse.

Jubilee head. Britannia on reverse .925 fine Silver, 16mm. Weight approx 1.87g

The Jubilee head 1888 issue was officially struck only for use in British Guiana. An example was not available at the time of writing to be weighed, so it is assumed that the weight of this coin is about the same as the previous young head issue.

Date	ESC	Mintage	Fine	VF	EF	UNC/BU
1888	1956		£7	£25	£50	£90/£100

GEORGE III .925 Fine Silver, 19mm. Weight 2.827g
The last coinage of George III (from 1816 - 1820) was designed by Benedetto Pistrucci. A big gap exists between sixpences, the previous coins struck for circulation were dated 1787.

Date	ESC	Mintage	Fine	VF	EF	UNC/BU
1816	1630	Inc with 1817	£7	£10	£50	£80/£110
1817	1632	10,921,680	£10	£18	£60	£80/£100
1818	1634	4,284,720	£10	£25	£70	£100/£120
1819	1636	4,712,400	£8	£20	£60	£80/£100
1819	1636A	Very small 8	£10	£20	£65	£80/£100
1819	ND	Noted with full stop after III.				
1820	1638	1,448,960	£8	£15	£60	£100/£120
1820	1639A	Upside-down 1 in date		£200	£500	£1000/

George III 1819 Sixpence

GEORGE IV Laureate first head .925 Fine Silver, 19mm. Weight 2.827g
The first George IV bust was by Benedetto Pistrucci. The reverses of the sixpences of George IV were basically smaller versions of the reverses used for the shillings. The first, used for 1821 only, featured a crowned ornate shield with a large rose under it. The second reverse, used 1824 to 1826 inclusive, featured a squarer shield with a circular garter surounding it, and no rose beneath. The third reverse, which is only found with the second obverse (the design by William Wyon) was a complete change and features a lion standing on a large crown.

First head with first reverse type.

Date	ESC	Mintage	Fine	VF	EF	UNC/BU
1821	1654	863,280	£10	£35	£90	£200/
1821	1656	BBITANNIAR error	£50	£145	£500	£700/£950
First head with second reverse type.						
1824	1657	633,600	£10	£20	£100	£225/
1825	1659	483,120	£10	£20	£80	£200/
1826	1660	689,040	£20	£55	£160	£280/£325
Bare second head with 3rd reverse type.						
1826	1662	Included above	£5	£15	£80	£180/
1827	1664	166,320	£12	£30	£80	£175/£220
1828	1665	15,840??	£9	£30	£100	£2000/
1829	1666	403,920	£12	£35	£120	£225/

George IV 1825 Sixpence
First head with second reverse

The changing reverse types of the George IV sixpences followed the same reverse types as the shillings. The first head was Laureate and very Roman in style, the second head was bare and more contemporary. The first reverse type is the ornate shield with a large crown. The second reverse was a much squarer shield surrounded by a garter (very similar to the Victorian Jubilee shilling reverse). The third reverse type was the large lion standing on a crown.

George IV 1826 Sixpence
Second head with third reverse

WILLIAM IV .925 Fine Silver, 19mm. Weight 2.827g
The William IV sixpences featured the familar William Wyon bust (from a model by Sir Francis Chantrey) and a new wreath type reverse by Jean Baptiste Merlen.

Date	ESC	Mintage	Fine	VF	EF	UNC/BU
1831	1670	1,340,195	£9	£25	£90	£180/
1834*	1674	5,892,480	£6	£25	£90	£200/
1835	1676	1,552,320	£15	£40	£100	£220/
1836	1678	1,987,920	£15	£35	£110	£220/
1837	1680	506,880	£15	£40	£100	£200/

William IV 1831 Sixpence

VICTORIA Young head .925 Fine Silver, 19mm. Weight 3.01g
The young head Victoria portrait, by William Wyon was changed slightly in 1867 and again in 1880. The reverse used was the same as that of William IV, although it was engraved by Leonard Charles Wyon, son of William. Coins dated 1864 to 1879 usually had a tiny die number on the reverse so that the mint staff could check the speed at which the dies became too worn or broken. Usually, what the die number happens to be has no bearing on the value of the coin, although some collectors do try to collect dates by die number.

Date	ESC	Mintage	Fine	VF	EF	UNC/BU
1838	1682	1,607,760	£10	£20	£55	£150/
1839	1684	3,310,560	£10	£25	£65	£150/
1840	1686	2,098,800	£8	£25	£55	£150/
1841	1687	1,386,000	£8	£24	£65	£160/
1842	1688	601,920	£8	£25	£70	£170/
1843	1689	3,160,080	£8	£26	£60	£160/
1844	1690	3,975,840	£8	£34	£100	£250/
1844	1690A	Date has large 44	£10	£35	£80	£220/
1845	1691	3,714,480	£8	£30	£80	£200/
1846	1692	4,268,880	£8	£20	£70	£200/
1848	1693	586,080	£35	£100	£325	£500/£600
1848	1693A	8 is altered 6	£35	£100	£325	£500/£600
1848	1693B	8 over 7	£35	£100	£325	£500/£600
1850	1695	498,960	£9	£20	£70	£200/£250
1850	1695A	5 struck over 3 (Cooke 1998)	£35	"GVF/VF"		
1851	1696	2,288,107	£9	£28	£75	£200/£250
1851	ND	Obv has one G with serif, one without. EF: £120				
1852	1697	904,586	£9	£30	£80	£200/£250
1853	ND	53 higher	(noted 2000) £70			
1853	1698	3,837,930	£9	£28	£75	£150/£200
1854	1700	840,116	£60	£275	£700	£1200/£1500
1855	1701	1,129,084	£9	£28	£80	£200/£285
1855	1701A	5 over 3. Slightly rarer than above.				
1856*	1702	2,779,920	£9	£28	£75	£180/£250
1857*	1704	2,233,440	£9	£28	£75	£170/£250
1858	1706	1,932,480	£10	£30	£75	£180/£250
1858	ND	2nd 8 over 6 (London Coins 2007)	£300			
1859	1708	4,688,640	£10	£28	£75	£180/£250

Victoria Young Head 1853 Sixpence

* 1834 - Rarer variety exists with date in large numerals (ESC1674A).

* 1856 and 1857 can also be found with a longer line below the word PENCE (ESC 1703 and 1705 respectively). Both varieties are as common as the normal coins.

VICTORIA Young head .925 Fine Silver, 19mm. Weight 3.0lg (continued)

Date	ESC	Mintage	Fine	VF	EF	UNC/BU
1859	1708A	9 struck over 8	£15	£40	£130	
1860	1709	1,100,880	£10	£20	£65	£160/£200
1862	1711	990,000	£25	£90	£300	£500/£600
1863	1712	491,040	£15	£60	£200	£300/£375

All Sixpences (except where stated) now have a small die number above the date until 1879.

Victoria Young Head 1885 Sixpence

Date	ESC	Mintage	Fine	VF	EF	UNC/BU
1864	1713	4,253,040	£12	£25	£95	£200/
1865	1714	1,631,520	£12	£25	£90	£200/
1866	1715	5,140,080	£12	£25	£90	£200/
1866	1716	No die number	£30	£120	£400	
1867	1717	1,362,240	£12	£30	£75	£190/
1868	1719	1,069,200	£12	£20	£80	£190/£250
1869	1720	388,080	£12	£20	£80	£190/£250
1870	1721	479,613	£12	£20	£90	£190/£250
1871	1723	3,662,684	£12	£20	£65	£160/£200
1871	1724	No die number	£20	£40	£130	£200/£250
1872	1726	3,382,048	£10	£25	£60	£150/£200
1873	1727	4,594,733	£12	£25	£60	£150/£200
1874	1728	4,225,726	£12	£25	£60	£150/
1875	1729	3,256,545	£12	£25	£60	£150/
1876	1730	841,435	£12	£30	£70	£170/£220
1877	1731	4,066,486	£10	£25	£60	£150/£200
1877	1732	No die number	£10	£25	£60	£140/£200
1878	1733	2,624,525	£10	£25	£60	£140/£200
1878	1734A	8 over 7	£50	£120	£280	
1878	ND	8 over 7, no die No.	£50	£150	£300	
1878	1735	DRITANNIAR error	£60	£130	£300	£500/£575
1879	1736	3,326,313	£10	£30	£70	£160/£220

Die numbers discontinued.

Date	ESC	Mintage	Fine	VF	EF	UNC/BU
1879	1737	Included above	£10	£20	£45	£120/
1880	ND	Hair lock on cheek	£15	£35	£80	£170/£200
1880*	1737C	No lock of hair	£9	£20	£50	£80/
1881	1740	6,239,447	£7	£15	£35	£90/£130
1882	1743	759,809	£12	£28	£70	£150/£180
1883	1744	4,986,558	£7	£18	£40	£120/
1884	1745	3,422,565	£6	£18	£40	£120/
1885	1746	4,652,771	£7	£18	£40	£120/
1886	1748	2,728,249	£7	£18	£45	£120/
1887	1750	3,675,607	£5	£18	£40	£130/

*The Young head Victoria portrait; to the untrained eye looks the same. There were however, minor changes made in 1867, and then again in 1880. The lock of hair on the cheek was removed during 1880 and that accounts for the two types that year.

Jubilee Head 1887 Sixpence.
The withdrawn type

Jubilee Head .925 Fine Silver, 19mm. Weight 3.0lg
The first type Jubilee head sixpence was quickly withdrawn due to it being of similar design to the roughly the same size half sovereign. At least one person was charged for gold plating a sixpence in order to pass it off as a half sovereign.

Reverse A: Gartered Shield, the withdrawn type.

Date	ESC	Mintage	Fine	VF	EF	UNC/BU
1887	1752	3,675,607	£2	£4	£10	£20/£26
1887	1752A	R of Victoria struck over I			£50	£100/£170
1887	1752B	JEB on truncation	£15	£30	£75	£125/£200
1887	1753	Proof				£70/£100

The B type Sixpences (on the next page) have a wreath reverse, just like that of the previous Young head Sixpence.

VICTORIA Jubilee Head, .925 Fine Silver, 19mm . Weight 3.0lg (continued)

Date	ESC	Mintage	Fine	VF	EF	UNC/BU
Reverse B: Crowned Value in Wreath.						
1887	1754	Included above	£3	£6	£10	£25/£30
1888	1756	4,197,698	£5	£8	£18	£50/£60
1889	1757	8,738,928	£5	£10	£18	£50/
1890	1758	9,386,955	£5	£10	£20	£50/
1891	1759	7,022,734	£5	£12	£20	£50/
1892	1760	6,245,746	£8	£12	£25	£60/
1893*	1761	7,350,619	£400	£600	£1400	

Victoria Veiled Head 1893 Sixpence obverse.
Reverse type as Edward VII sixpence.

* Noted: £225 Fair/Near Fair (R. Ingram Coins 2005)
£130 VG/Near VG (London Coins 2006)

VICTORIA Old or Widow Head, .925 Fine Silver, 19mm. Weight 3.0lg
Portrait by Thomas Brock, engraved by George William de Saulles. The reverse was a slightly modified version of the original Jean Baptiste Merlen design.

Date	ESC	Mintage	Fine	VF	EF	UNC/BU
1893	1762	Included above	£4	£5	£20	£35/£50
1894	1764	3,467,704	£6	£10	£28	£50/£65
1895	1765	7,024,631	£5	£10	£24	£45/£60
1896	1766	6,651,699	£5	£10	£24	£35/£45
1897	1767	5,031,498	£5	£10	£24	£35/£45
1898	1768	5,914,100	£5	£10	£24	£40/£60
1899	1769	7,996,804	£5	£10	£24	£40/£60
1900	1770	8,984,354	£8	£10	£30	£40/£60
1901	1771	5,108,757	£5	£9	£20	£30/£50

EDWARD VII .925 Fine Silver, 19mm. Weight 3.0lg
From this reign onwards the use of a reducing machine was adopted. Usually one person was responsible for the large design and the old job of creating a smaller version to strike coins is now undertaken mechanically. The engraver being made quite redundant in this respect! George William de Saulles was responsible for the Edward VII portrait and the reverse was a modified version of the previous old head Victoria type.

Date	ESC	Mintage	Fine	VF	EF	UNC/BU
1902	1785	6,367,378	£3	£6	£15	£50/£75
1902	1786	15,123 Proofs with matt finish				£24/£35
1903	1787	5,410,096	£8	£15	£50	£75/£100
1904	1788	4,487,098	£9	£20	£65	£110/£150
1905	1789	4,235,556	£9	£20	£70	£120/£160
1906	1790	7,641,146	£8	£15	£35	£75/£100
1907	1791	8,733,673	£8	£15	£35	£75/£100
1908	1792	6,739,491	£8	£15	£35	£80/£100
1909	1793	6,584,017	£8	£15	£35	£80/£100
1910	1794	12,490,724	£5	£9	£25	£45/£60

Edward VII 1906 Sixpence

GEORGE V .925 Fine Silver (until 1920) 19mm. Weight 3.01g
The bust was by Bertram MacKennal, the reverse was a smaller version of that used for the shilling, which was esentially a modified version of that used for the Edward VII shilling and designed originally by de Saulles.

Date	ESC	Mintage	Fine	VF	EF	UNC/BU
1911	1795	9,155,310	£2	£5	£18	£25/£35
1911	1796	6,007 Proofs				£35/£50
1912	1797	10,984,129	£2	£6	£25	£45/£60
1913	1798	7,499,833	£2	£9	£32	£60/£70
1914	1799	22,714,602	£2	£5	£15	£40/£50
1915	1800	15,694,597	£2	£5	£15	£40/£50
1916	1801	22,207,178	£2	£5	£10	£25/£40
1917	1802	7,725,475	£3	£12	£35	£65/£75
1918	1803	27,558,743	£2	£5	£15	£35/£50
1919	1804	13,375,447	£2	£4	£18	£35/£50
1920	1805	14,136,287. Ag .925	£3	£8	£25	£60/£70

George V 1926 Sixpence. 1st reverse type.
Early (1st Effigy) sixpences have
a slightly larger bust.

GEORGE V Now debased to .500 Silver, 19mm. Weight 2.876g

Date	ESC	Mintage	Fine	VF	EF	UNC/BU
1920	1806	Silver .500	£2	£4	£15	£30/£45
1921	1807	30,339,741	£2	£4	£15	£25/£35
1922	1808	16,878,890	£2	£4	£20	£20/£30
1923	1809	6,382,793	£2	£4	£20	£35/£50
1924	1810	17,444,218	£1	£4	£20	£35/£45
1925	1811	12,720,558	£1	£5	£16	£40/£50
1925	1812	With new broader rim	£2	£4	£11	£30/£40
1926	1813	21,809,261	£1	£5	£18	£45/£60
1926	1814	Modified Effigy (Ap 1)	£1	£5	£10	£35/£50
1927	1815	68,939,873	£1	£2	£10	£35/£45
1927	1816	15,000 Proofs.New Oak/Acorn reverse				£35/£40
1928	1817	23,123,384		£2	£10	£28/£38
1929	1818	28,319,326		£2	£10	£25/£35
1930	1819	16,990,289		£2	£15	£25/£35
1931**	1820	16,873,268	£1	£5	£20	£30/£40
1932	1821	9,406,117	£2	£4	£12	£30/£45
1933	1822	22,185,083	£2	£5	£9	£30/£40
1934	1823	9,304,009	£2	£5	£10	£30/£40
1935	1824	13,995,621		£1	£6	£25/£35
1936	1825	24,380,171		£1	£5	£25/£35

George V 1934 Sixpence.
2nd reverse type

** The later George V Sixpences from 1931 onwards have finer edge millings.

EDWARD VIII .500 Silver 19mm
The reverse featuring six linked rings of St. Edmund designed by George Kruger Gray. The obverse was by Thomas Humphrey Paget. Like all Edward VIII coins, this was not officially issued.

Date	ESC	Mintage	Fine	VF	EF	UNC/BU
1937	1825B	3 or 4 known	Approximately			£30,000

(last known sale was in 1997. An AFDC coin for £12,000)

GEORGE VI .500 Silver (until 1946) 19mm. Weight 2.827g
The obverse portrait of all George VI coins was by Thomas Humphrey Paget. The reverse is by George Kruger Gray.
From 1947 the silver content was completely removed and the new coins were made from a copper and nickel alloy
(Cupro-Nickel). In 1949 the King gave up his IND:IMP (Emperor of India) title due to that countries new indepen-
dence. Partly in order to fill the space this left, the reverse was redesigned to use a different monogram.

Date	ESC	Mintage	EF	UNC/BU
1937	1826	22,302,524	£2	£7/£5
1937	1827	26,402 Proofs		£7/£10
1938	1828	13,402,701	£3	£18/£30
1939	1829	28,670,304	£2	£10/£15
1940	1830	20,875,196	£2	£10/£15
1941	1831	23,186,616	£2	£10/£15
1942	1832	44,942,785	£1	£10/£15
1943	1833	46,927,111	£1	£8/£15
1944	1834	37,952,600	£1	£8/£15
1945	1835	39,939,259	£1	£8/£14
1946	1836	43,466,407	£1	£8/£14

George VI 1939 Sixpence.
1st reverse

GEORGE VI Cupro-Nickel (No silver), 19mm. Weight 2.81g
(weights seem to be slightly more for the new monogram type, 1949 - 1952)

Date	ESC	Mintage	EF	UNC/BU
1947	1837	29,993,263	£1	£6/£7
1948	1838	88,323,540		£6/£7
1949*	1838A	41,355,515	£1	£6/£8
1950	1838B	32,741,955	£2	£9/£15
1950	1838C	17,513 Proofs		£10/£15
1951	1838D	40,399,491	£3	£7/£14
1951	1838E	20,000 Proofs	£4	£10/£15
1952	1838F	1,013,477	VF:£10 £30	£80/£150

George VI Sixpence
2nd reverse used from 1949 - 52.

ELIZABETH II Cupro-Nickel (No silver), 19mm . Weight 2.83g
Portrait by Mary Gillick, reverse is by Edgar Fuller, modeled by Cecil Thomas. From 1954 the title BRITT OMN
was omitted. All ESC numbers start with 1838, followed by the letter shown.

Date	ESC	Mintage	EF	UNC/BU
1953	H	70,323,876	50p	£2/£3
1953	G	40,000 Proofs		£3/£5
1954*	I	105,241,150	£1	£4/£5
1955	J	109,929,554	20p	£6/£8
1956	K	109,841,555	20p	£4/£5
1957	L	105,654,290	20p	£3/£4
1958	M	123,518,527		£5/£6
1959	N	93,089441		£1/£2
1960	O	103,288,346		£5/£6
1961	P	115,052,017		£5/£6
1962	Q	178,359,637		£2/£3
1963	R	112,964,000		£3/£4
1964	S	152,336,000		£1/£2
1965	T	129,644,000		£1/£2
1966	U	175,696,000		50p/£1
1967	V	240,788,000		30p/70p
1970	W	750,476 Proofs		£2/£3

Elizabeth II 1955 Sixpence

GEORGE III .925 Fine silver, around 23.5mm. Weight 5.65g
The last major issue of shillings for circulation was in 1787. During the latter part of the 18th century captured Spanish colonial silver coins were circulating in Great Britain due to the lack of proper silver coinage. In 1797 the government made this more official by countermarking Spanish colonial coins and making them legal tender for various face values. It wasn't until 1816/17 that a proper re-coinage was undertaken at the new Royal Mint building at Tower Hill, which was fully equipped with the new and proven Boulton/Watt technology (see notes for Cartwheel Twopence). One of the first coins to be struck was the shilling, which interestingly, remained legal tender as 1/20th of a pound sterling until the decimal equivalent (the 5p) was made smaller in 1990. The portrait of George III was the work of Benedetto Pistrucci, as was the reverse. The dies were cut by Thomas Wyon.

Date	ESC	Mintage	Fine	VF	EF	UNC/BU
1816	1228		£6	£15	£35	£80/£100
1817	1232	23,031,360	£6	£14	£30	£75/£95
1817	1232A	2nd E of GEORGE over R			£150+	
1817	ND	RRIT Error		£60	£100	
1818	1234	1,342,440	£20	£40	£100	£200/
1818	1234A	2nd 8 higher	£30	£60	£165	£300/
1819	1235	7,595,280	£8	£25	£80	£130/
1819	ND	9 over 6			£220	
1819	1235A	9 over 8	£20	£50	£150	£300/
1820	1236	7,975,440	£10	£22	£35	£80/£120
1820	1236A	1 of HONI over S		£60	£150	£250/
1820	ND	H of HONI over sideways H			£500/	

George III 1816 Shilling

GEORGE IV .925 Fine Silver, just over 23mm. Weight 5.65g
The first George IV bust was by Benedetto Pistrucci. The obverses and reverses used were the same as the sixpences. The first, used for 1821 only, featured a crowned ornate shield with a large rose under it. The second reverse, used 1823 to 1825, featured a squarer shield with a circular garter surrounding it, and no rose beneath. The third reverse, which is only found with the second obverse (the design by William Wyon) was a complete change and features a lion standing on a large crown.

The first Laureate Head of George IV,
shown with the first and second reverse types.

GEORGE IV .925 Fine silver, around 23.5mm. Weight 5.65g

Date	ESC	Mintage	Fine	VF	EF	UNC/BU
1st Head - Laureate Roman style, 1st Reverse shield.						
1821	1247	2,463,120		£10	£40	£160	£300/
1st Head - Laureate Roman style, 2nd Rev shield.						
1823	1249	693,000	£40	£200	£600	
1824	1251	4,158,000	£10	£50	£150	£300/
1825	1253	2,459,160	£15	£45	£150	£300/
1825	1253B	5 struck over 3	£150			
2nd head - Bare type, 3rd Rev with large lion and crown.						
1825	1254	Inc above	£9	£32	£90	£250/
1825	1254A	1 for 1 in date. Fine: £495 (R Ingram 2006)				
1826	1257	6,351,840	£8	£20	£70	£200/
1826	1257A	6/2	£9	£20	£80	£200/
1827	1259	574,200	£25	£75	£200	£370/
1829	1260	879,120	£20	£50	£100	£220/

The second (bare) head and its only reverse (the third George IV shilling reverse)

WILLIAM IV .925 Fine silver, just over 23mm. Weight 5.65g
A larger version of the sixpence, the William IV shilling featured the familar William Wyon bust (from a model by Sir Francis Chantrey) and wreath type reverse by Jean Baptiste Merlen.

Date	ESC	Mintage	Fine	VF	EF	UNC/BU
1834	1268	3,223,440	£10	£40	£130	£300/
1835	1271	1,449,360	£18	£45	£130	£300/
1836	1273	3,567,960	£18	£45	£130	£300/
1837	1276	479,160	£25	£100	£350	
1837	ND	R over low A (noted 2003) "AFDC"				£400/

William IV Shilling obverse.
The reverse used was the wreath type, as with Young Head Victorian Shillings.

VICTORIA .925 Fine silver, around 23.5mm. Weight 5.65g
The Young Head design was the work of William Wyon, the reverse used was basically that used previously for William IV. A few minor changes were made to the bust to age it, although it looked pretty similar even 50 years into the reign, when it was replaced by the Jubilee bust. Small die numbers were used on the reverse for dates indicated.

Date	ESC	Mintage	Fine	VF	EF	UNC/BU
1st Young Head						
1838	1278	W.W. 1,956,240	£12	£20	£100	£200/
1839	1280	W.W. 5,666,760	£10	£18	£80	£170/
2nd Young Head (minor differences).						
1839	1283	No W.W. at neck	£10	£25	£120	£220/
1840	1285	1,639,440	£15	£50	£140	£250/
1841	1287	875,160	£12	£35	£125	£200/
1842	1288	2,094,840	£12	£35	£80	£180/
1843	1290	1,465,200	£12	£40	£150	£250/
1844	1291	4,466,880	£12	£35	£90	£190/
1845	1292	4,082,760	£10	£35	£90	£220/
1846	1293	4,031,280	£10	£35	£100	£200/£280
1848	ND	1,041,480 (More common with 8/6)			£350 EF approx.	
1848	1294	2nd 8 over 6	£60	£100	£300	£500/£600
1849	1295	645,480	£10	£40	£100	£220/
1850	1296	685,080	£400			
1850	ND	50 over 46		£400		
1850	1297	50 over 49	£125	£450	£1500	
1851	1298	470,071	£30	£75	£250	£450/
1852	1299	1,306,574	£15	£35	£100	£220/
1853	1300	4,256,188	£15	£35	£100	£220/
1854	1302	552,414	£250	£500		
1854	1302A	4 over 1	£200		£1500	
1855	1303	1,368,499	£12	£35	£85	£200/
1856	1304	3,168,000	£10	£35	£130	£275/
1857	1305	2,562,120	£10	£30	£90	£180/
1857	1305A	Inverted G in DG	£125	£250	£450	
1858	1306	3,108,600	£10	£30	£85	£180/
1858	ND	8 over 8		NEF	£120 Approx	
1859	1307	4,561,920	£8	£26	£75	£170/
1859	ND	9 over 8 (or ??) NF: £95 (R Ingram 2006)				
1860	1308	1,671,120	£10	£25	£70	£200/
1861	1309	1,382,040	£15	£40	£100	£250/
1861	ND	1 over tilted 1 Approx			£200	£320/
1862	1310	954,360	£35	£100		
1863	1311	859,320	£30	£80	£200	£300/£325
1863	1311A	3 over 1	£90	£230	£320/	
All shillings (except where stated) now have a small die number above the date until 1879.						
1864	1312	4,518,360	£6	£20	£100	£200/
1865	1313	5,619,240	£6	£20	£100	£200/
1866	1314	4,989,600	£6	£20	£100	£200/£200
1866	1314A	BBITANNIAR error (Noted: 1995) 'EF' £350				
1867	1315	2,166,120	£6	£15	£45	£150/£200

Victoria Young head 1839 Shilling

VICTORIA .925 Fine silver, around 23.5mm. Weight 5.65g (continued)

3rd Young Head (minor differences).

Date	ESC	Mintage	Fine	VF	EF	UNC/BU
1867*	1316		£50	£100	£400	
1868	1318	3,330,360	£8	£20	£75	£170/£200
1869	1319	736,560	£12	£25	£90	£180/
1870	1320	1,467,471	£12	£25	£90	£180/
1871	1321	4,910,010	£10	£25	£80	£160/
1872	1324	8,897,781	£10	£25	£80	£160/
1872	ND	Raised dot between R and A in GRATIA. NVF: £50				
1873	1325	6,489,598	£8	£20	£65	£120/£160
1874	1326	5,503,747	£8	£20	£65	£120/£160
1874	ND	With crosslet 4	£35	£75	£150/	
1875	1327	4,353,983	£8	£20	£75	£150/£175
1876	1328	1,057,487	£8	£25	£60	£100/£125
1877*	1329	2,980,703	£6	£15	£65	£120/
1878	1330	3,127,131	£5	£15	£70	£120/
1878		As above with die number 1			£250/	
1878	ND	Last R in BRITANNIAR over A. Reported 2006.				
1879	1332	3,611,507	£30	£120		

4th Young Head (slightly older features and other minor differences).

Date	ESC	Mintage	Fine	VF	EF	UNC/BU
1879	1334	No die no.	£8	£20	£100	£200/
1880	1335	4,842,786	£6	£20	£80	£200/
1881*	1338	5,255,332	£6	£22	£75	£200/
1882	1341	1,611,786	£12	£35	£120	£220/
1883	1342	7,281,4.50	£8	£30	£70	£200/
1884	1343	3,923,993	£8	£12	£30	£95/
1885	1345	3,336,527	£7	£10	£35	£120/
1886	1347	2,086,819	£7	£12	£40	£90/
1887	1349	4,034,133 YH	£15	£28	£85	£140/

* 1867 with the third lower relief Young head has not been confirmed to exist. 1877 is also believed to exist without a die number. 1881 has a variety with a shorter line under the word SHILLING (ESC 1338A). Both varieties are thought to be equally common.

Victoria Jubilee head 1887 Shilling

VICTORIA Jubilee Head type .925 Fine silver, around 23.5mm . Weight 5.65g
Sir Joseph Boehm designed the Jubilee head, which was engraved by Leonard Charles Wyon. Mr Wyon also engraved the reverse, but from his own design. In 1889 the head was made slightly larger. The old head bust was by Sir Thomas Brock, the reverse of the old head shilling was by Sir Edward Poynter. Both sides of the old head shilling were engraved by George William de Saulles.

Date	ESC	Mintage	Fine	VF	EF	UNC/BU
1887*	1351	Included above	£1	£4	£7	£30/£50
1887	1352	1,312 Proofs			£65/£75	
1888	1353	4,526,856 Last 8/7	£5	£10	£25	£90/£160
1889	1354	7,039,628 small head	£30	£85	£275	£365/£450
1889	1355	Larger head	£4	£11	£30	£100/
1890	1357	8,794,042	£4	£11	£40	£60/£75
1891	1358	5,565,348	£5	£15	£45	£90/
1892	1360	4,591,622	£5	£15	£45	£90/£170

1887 - Varieties with the device that divides the '18' and '87'.

The device pointing to a rim tooth is scarcer than when the device points between two rim teeth.

Old, Veiled or Widow Head type. Weight 5.65g:

Date	ESC	Mintage	Fine	VF	EF	UNC/BU
1893	1361	7,039,074	£4	£9	£20	£75/£100
1893	1361A	Small letters Obv	£5	£12	£30	£100/
1893	1362	1,312 Proofs			£60/£85	
1894	1363	5,953,152	£6	£10	£40	£100/
1895	1364	8,880,651 Small rose	£10	£20	£40	£80/£100
1895	1364A	Larger rose on Rev	£4	£12	£20	£50/£65
1896	1365	9,264,551 Large rose	£4	£10	£20	£45/£60
1896	1365A	Smaller rose on Rev	£10	£20	£40	£70/£100
1897	1366	6,270,364	£4	£10	£20	£40/£60
1898	1367	9,768,703	£4	£10	£25	£65/£100
1899	1368	10,965,382	£4	£10	£16	£35/£50
1900	1369	10,937,590	£4	£12	£15	£30/£55
1901	1370	3,426,294	£5	£12	£20	£50/£70

Victoria Veiled head 1895 Shilling

EDWARD VII .925 Fine silver, 23.6mm. Weight 5.65g
Both the obverse and reverse were designed and engraved by George William de Saulles.

Date	ESC	Mintage	Fine	VF	EF	UNC/BU
1902	1410	7,809,481	£5	£9	£35	£65/£75
1902	1411	15,123 Proofs with matt finish				£60/£75
1903	1412	2,061,823	£8	£20	£100	£250/
1904	1413	2,040,161	£10	£25	£90	£220/
1905	1414	488,390	£70	£160	£700	
1906	1415	10,791,025	£4	£15	£70	£150/
1907	1416	4,083,418	£6	£20	£50	£125/£200
1908	1417	3,806,969	£10	£20	£90	£200/
1909	1418	5,664,982	£15	£75	£150	£260/
1910	1419	26,547,236	£3	£8	£40	£80/£100

Forgeries exist of 1905 shillings.

GEORGE V .925 Fine silver (until 1920), 23.6mm. Weight 5.65g
Bust by Sir Bertram MacKennal, reverse as Edward VII type.

Edward VII 1910 Shilling

Date	ESC	Mintage	Fine	VF	EF	UNC/BU
1911*	1420	20,065,901	£3	£6	£20	£35/£40
1911	1421	6,007 Proofs				£50/£70
1912**	1422	15,594,009	£3	£11	£35	£60/
1913	1423	9,011,509	£4	£15	£35	£70/£100
1914	1424	23,415,843	£2	£5	£25	£40/£60
1915	1425	39,279,024		£4	£20	£40/£50
1916	1426	35,862,015		£4	£16	£35/£50
1917	1427	22,202,608		£5	£20	£40/£50
1918	1428	34,915,934		£5	£15	£30/£40
1919	1429	10,823,824	£5	£9	£30	£55/£65

Reduced to .500 silver, size and weight as above.

Date	ESC	Mintage	Fine	VF	EF	UNC/BU
1920	1430	22,825,142	£1	£5	£15	£45/£55
1921	1431	22,648,763	£1	£8	£20	£55/£65
1922	1432	27,215,738	£1	£4	£25	£40/£50
1923	1433	14,575,243	£2	£4	£12	£30/£35
1924	1434	9,250,095	£1	£6	£18	£35/£40
1925	1435	5,418,764	£1	£12	£50	£100/
1926	1436	22,516,453	£1	£4	£15	£30/£40
1926	1437	Mod Effigy (see Appendix I) £1	£3	£10	£35/£45
1927	1438	9,262,344	£1	£5	£15	£35/£50

George V 1915 1st type Shilling, 1911-26. The reverse is almost identical to the Edward VII reverse.

* Obv I: Above B.M. the neck is hollow.
Obv 2: Above B.M. the neck is flat.
Reverse A: 'I' in GEORGIVS
points between 2 beads.
Reverse B: 'I' in GEORGIVS points at a bead.

1911 has been reported with combinations of the above obverse and reverses.

**1912 has been reported with the 'IMP' closely spaced and widely spaced: 'I M P'.

GEORGE V .925 Fine silver (until 1920), 23.6mm. Weight 5.65g
New design with no inner circle and the date to the right. Obverse by MacKennel,
reverse by George Kruger Gray.

Date	ESC	Mintage	Fine	VF	EF	UNC/BU
1927	1439	New design	£1	£3	£12	£22/£30
1927	1440	15,000 Proofs				£30/£45
1928	1441	18,136,778		£1	£5	£22/£30
1929	1442	19,343,006		£1	£5	£20/£30
1930	1443	3,137,092	£2	£6	£20	£40/£60
1931	1444	6,993,926		£2	£6	£20/£30
1932	1445	12,168,101		£2	£10	£25/£35
1933	1446	11,511,624		£2	£6	£20/£30
1934	1447	6,138,463		£5	£10	£30/£40
1935	1448	9,183,462		£2	£10	£20/£25
1936	1449	11,910,613		£2	£10	£20/£25

EDWARD VIII, .500 silver, just over 23mm
The reverse was the George VI Scottish type designed by George Kruger Gray.
The obverse was by Thomas Humphrey Paget. Like all Edward VIII coins, this was
not officially issued.

Date	ESC	Mintage	Fine	VF	EF	UNC/BU
1936	1449B	Pattern Scottish type only		'Guesstimate'		£30,000

George V 1929 2nd type Shilling. 1927-36

George VI 1942 English type Shilling

GEORGE VI .500 silver (until 1947), just over 23mm. Weight 5.6lg
The reverses were by George Kruger Gray. The obverse was by Thomas Humphrey Paget.

Date	ESC	Mintage	EF	UNC/BU
1937E	1450	8,359,122	£2	£9/£12
1937E	1451	Proof 26,402		£8/£10
1937S	1452	6,748,875	£2	£7/£9
1937S	1453	Proof 26,402		£5/£8
1938E	1454	4,833,436	£6	£9/£15
1938S	1455	4,797,852	£6	£9/£15
1939E	1456	11,052,677	£6	£10/£12
1939S	1457	10,263,892	£6	£10/£12
1940E	1458	11,099,126	£5	£10/£12
1940S	1459	9,913,089	£4	£9/£11
1941E	1460	11,391,883	£2	£10/£12
1941S	1461	8,086,030	£2	£8/£10
1942E	1462	17,453,643	£1	£10/£12
1942S	1463	13,676,759	£1	£8/£10
1943E	1464	11,404,213	£1	£7/£10
1943S	1465	9,824,214	£1	£7/£10
1944E	1466	11,586,752	£1	£7/£10
1944S	1467	10,990,167	£1	£7/£10
1945E	1468	15,143,404	£1	£7/£8
1945S	1469	15,106,270	£1	£7/£8
1946E	1470	18,663,797 **	£1	£6/£7
1946S	1471	16,381,501	£1	£6/£7

Cupro-Nickel (no silver) Type as before. Weight 5.68g

1947E	1472	12,120,611	£1	£7/£8
1947S	1473	12,282,223	£1	£7/£8
1948E	1474	45,576,923	£1	£7/£8
1948S	1475	45,351,937	£1	£7/£8

IND : IMP in legend discontinued.

1949E	1475A	19,328,405	£2	£10/£12
1949S	1475B	21,243,074	£2	£10/£12
1950E	1475C	19,243,872	£5	£10/£15
1950E	1475D	17,513 Proofs	FDC	£16
1950S	1475E	14,299,601	£5	£15/£17
1950S	1475F	17,513 Proofs	FDC	£17
1951E	1475G	9,956,930	£2	£10/£12
1951E	1475H	20,000 Proofs	FDC	£17
1951S	1475I	10,961,174	£2	£8/£10
1951S	1475J	20,000 Proofs	FDC	£15
1952E	1475*	1 known outside of the Royal Collection.		

From 1937 - 1966 (and again for the 1970 proofs) Shillings were struck with either an English or Scottish reverse type. They circulated, generally, throughout the United Kingdom and are indicated in this book by the suffix E or S after the date.

George VI Scottish type Shilling reverse

** 1946E has been reported with two reverse varieties concerning the pointing of the 'IND'.
Reverse A: The 'I' points to a rim bead. Reverse B: The 'I' points between two beads.

Like with a lot of minor varieties on common coins, this is rarely distinguished and the values are assumed to be the same.

ELIZABETH II, Cupro-Nickel (no silver), 23.6mm. Weight 5.63g
The young Elizabeth portrait was designed by Mary Gillick. The English and Scottish reverse types were by William
Gardner. As with all the Elizabeth II coins, the BRITT OMN was removed in 1954. All the shillings below have the
ESC number 1475 followed by the letter(s) shown.

Date	ESC	Mintage	EF	UNC/BU
1953E	K	41,942,894	50p	£2/£3
1953	ND	Head both sides.		£300/
		Undated but BRITT:OMN present		
1953E	L	Proofs 40,000	FDC	£10
1953S	M	20,663,528	50p	£2/£3
1953S	N	40,000 Proofs	FDC	£6
1954E	O	30,262,032	£1	£5/£7
1954S	P	26,771,735	£1	£7/£9
1955E	Q	45,259,908	£1	£9/£12
1955S	R	27,950,906	£1	£8/£10
		Also exists with broader rim.		
1956E	S	44,907,008	£3	£11/£15
1956S	T	42,853,637	£2	£10/£14
1957E	U	42,774,217	£1	£8/£10
1957S	V	17,959,988	£3	£15/£18
1958E	W	14,392,305	3	£12/£15
1958S	X	40,822,557	50p	£3/£4
1959E	Y	19,442,778	£1	£4/£8
1959S	Z	1,012,988	£3	£12/£18
1960E	AA	27,027,914	£1	£5/£7
1960S	BB	14,376,932	£1	£5/£7
1961E	CC	39,816,907	50p	£4/£6
1961S	DD	2,762,558	£1	£5/£7
1962E	EE	36,704,379		£4/£6
1962S	FF	18,967,310		£4/£6
1963E	GG	44,714,000		£2/£3
1963S	HH	32,300,000		£2/£3
1964E	II	8,590,900		£2/£3
1964S	JJ	5,239,100		£2/£6
1965E	KK	9,218,000		£1/£2
1965S	LL	2,774,000		£1/£2
1966E	MM	15,005,000 *		£1/£2
1966S	NN	15,607,000 *		£1/£2
1966S		Wrong alignment **		£70/£100
1970E	OO	Proofs 750,476 from set		£2/£4
1970S	PP	Proofs 750,476 from set		£2/£4

Elizabeth II 1965 Scottish type Shilling

The Elizabeth II English type reverse

* Mintage number includes some struck in 1967, but dated 1966.
** Coin struck with incorrect 'Coin' alignment, see appendix I.

Eighteenpence Bank tokens (One Shilling and Sixpence)

This interesting series, issued under the authority of the Bank of England was really an authorised token issue providing much needed change until the major re-coinage of 1816. Two bust types were used on these during their short date run. The first bust is the military type as illustrated, the second bust was a not entirely attractive laureate head type.

GEORGE III .925 Fine Silver, 26mm. Weight, about 7.3g

Date	ESC	Details	F	VF	EF	UNC/BU
1811	969		£9	£18	£36	£130/
1812	971	(1st head)	£9	£18	£36	£130/
1812	972	(2nd head)	£8	£16	£32	£100/
1813	976		£8	£16	£32	£100/
1814	977		£8	£16	£32	£100/
1815	978		£8	£16	£32	£100/
1816	979		£8	£16	£32	£100/

Florins / Two Shillings

Second head Eighteenpence Bank Token of 1814

VICTORIA .925 fine silver, 28mm. Weight 11.31g. The Godless Florin.
During a time when religion was more widely practised and being a good Christian was a focal point of most peoples lives, it was probably asking for trouble to produce a coin for circulation omitting the words 'DEI GRATIA' (For the grace of god). Even though it was pretty revolutionary, being one tenth of a pound, and therefore Britains first decimal coin, it didn't last long, and was replaced two years later by a redesigned 'Gothic' style florin. William Wyon designed both obverses and William Dyce was responsible for both reverses. Confusingly for novices, the Gothic florins have no numerical date on them, instead, it is in Roman Numerals after the obverse legend.

Date	ESC	Mintage	Roman Date	Fine	VF	EF	UNC/BU
1849	802	413,830		£20	£35	£120	£160/£250
1849	802A	'WW' initials partly obliterated		£40	£180	£300/£350	

VICTORIA .925 fine silver, 30mm. Weight approx 11.35g. The Gothic Florin.

Date	ESC	Mintage	Roman Date	Fine	VF	EF	UNC/BU
1851	803	1,540	mdcccli	£2000+	(reported 1995)		
1852	806	1,014,552	mdccclii	£20	£70	£140	£250/
1852	807A	ii struck over i				£400/	
1853	807B	3,919,950	mdcccliii	£15	£60	£160	£250/
1853	808	With no stop after date.		£15	£60	£140	£250/
1854	811	550,413	mdcccliv	£400	£700	£1800	
1855	812	831,017	mdccclv	£20	£60	£140	£350/
1856	813	2,201,760	mdccclvi	£15	£40	£180	£350/
1856	813A	With no stop after date.		£15	£75	£200	£350/
1857	814	1,671,120	mdccclvii	£15	£50	£200	£350/
1858	816	2,239,380	mdccclviii	£18	£50	£200	£300/
1858	816B	With no stop after date.		£18	£40	£140	£250/
1859	817	2,568,060	mdccclvix	£22	£70	£220	£360/£450
1859	818	With no stop after date.	Rare				

Victoria 1849 'Godless' Florin

VICTORIA .925 fine silver, 30mm. Weight approx 11.35g. The Gothic Florin

Date	ESC	Mintage	Roman Date	Fine	VF	EF	UNC/BU
1860	819	1,475,100	mdccclx	£18	£70	£200	£350/
1862	820	594,000	mdccclxii	£100	£500		
1863	822	938,520	mdccclxiii	£1000			
1864	824	1,861,200	mdccclxiv	£20	£75	£200	
1865	826	1,580,044	mdccclxv	£25	£75	£200	
1866	828	914,760	mdccclxvi	£20	£85	£220	
1866	829	With colon after date.		Rare			
1867	830	423,720	mdccclxvii	£20	£65	£200	£400/
1867	832A	No 'WW' (42 arcs in border)		Extremely rare			
1868	833	896,940	mdccclxviii	£15	£50	£200	
1869	834	297,000	mdccclxix	£50	£100	£300	
1870	836	1,080,648	mdccclxx	£50	£100	£300	
1871	837	3,425,605	mdccclxxi	£15	£55	£150	£250/
1872	840	7,199,690	mdccclxxii	£15	£55	£160	£300/
1873	841	5,921,839	mdccclxxiii	£15	£55	£150	£250/
1874	843	1,642,630	mdccclxxiv	£20	£80	£200	£350/
1874	843A	iv struck over iii		£25	£60	(noted	1999)
1875	844	1,117,030	mdccclxxv	£15	£50	£150	£250/
1876	845	580,034	mdccclxxvi	£40	£100		£350/
1877	846	682,292	mdccclxxvii	£15	£50	£150	£280/
1877	847	No 'WW' (48 arcs in border)		£50	£120	£240	
1877	848	No 'WW' (42 arcs in border)		£20	£60	£200	
1878	849	1,786,680	mdccclxxviii	£15	£40	£150	£280/
1879	1,512,247		mdccclxxix :				
	849B	Die No. present, 48 arcs		£30	£75	£200	(with WW)
	850	42 border arcs		£100	£200	(no WW initials)	
	851	No Die No. 48 border arcs		£15	£50	£180	£300/
	852	38 border arcs		£20	£65	£200	
1880	854A	Portrait as 1868-1877. It's difficult to tell the difference between this and the normal 1880 coin below. This type is extremely rare.					
1880	854	2,167,170	mdccclxxx	£20	£50	£150	£250/
1881	856	2,570,337	mdccclxxxi	£20	£60	£150	£280/
1881	858A	Broken die, last 'x' looks like an 'r'			£300	£650/	
1883	859	3,555,667	mdccclxxxiii	£15	£50	£110	£220/
1884	860	1,447,379	mdccclxxxiv	£15	£50	£120	£250/
1885	861	1,758,210	mdccclxxxv	£18	£50	£120	£250/
1886	863	591,773	mdccclxxxvi	£15	£45	£120	£250/
1887	865	1,776,903	mdccclxxxvii	£15	£50	£130	£280/
1887	866	'WW' present (46 arcs in border)		£50	£170	£340/	

Victoria 1864 'Gothic' Florin

VICTORIA .925 fine silver, Jubilee Head type 29.5mm. Weight approx 11.3g.
Sir Joseph Boehm designed the Jubilee head, which was engraved by Leonard Charles Wyon. Mr Wyon also engraved the reverse, but from his own design. The old head bust was by Sir Thomas Brock, the reverse of the old head florin was by Sir Edward Poynter. Both sides of the old head florin were engraved by George William de Saulles.

Date	ESC	Mintage	Fine	VF	EF	UNC/BU
1887	868	Included with Gothic	£3	£7	£22	£40/£70
1887	869	1,084 Jubilee Head Proofs			£40	£80/£125
1888	870	1,541,540	£8	£15	£50	£100/
1889	871	2,973,561	£7	£15	£40	£80/
1890	872	1,684,737	£10	£45	£100	
1891	873	836,438	£30	£60	£100	£160/£250
1892	874	283,401	£30	£75	£250	

VICTORIA .925 fine silver, Veiled or Widow Head 28.5mm. Weight approx 11.3g.

Date	ESC	Mintage	Fine	VF	EF	UNC/BU
1893	876	1,666,103	£4	£9	£50	£100/£130
1894	878	1,952,842	£5	£12	£70	£110/£140
1895	879	2,182,968	£5	£10	£50	£110/£140
1896	880	2,944,416	£5	£10	£50	£80/£100
1897	881	1,699,921	£5	£10	£65	£100/£130
1898	882	3,061,343	£5	£10	£40	£80/£100
1899	883	3,966,953	£4	£10	£40	£80/£100
1900	884	5,528,630	£6	£20	£60	£85/£100
1901	885	2,648,870	£4	£12	£50	£100/£130

Victoria Jubilee Head 1887 Florin

EDWARD VII .925 fine silver, 28.5mm. Weight approx 11.3g.
Both the obverse and reverse were designed and engraved by George William de Saulles.

Date	ESC	Mintage	Fine	VF	EF	UNC/BU
1902	919	2,489,575	£10	£20	£40	£85/£120
1902	920	15,123 Matt finish Proofs				£70/£85
1903	921	1,995,298	£15	£60	£120	£200/
1904	922	2,769,932	£15	£55	£150	£300/
1905	923	1,187,596	£50	£170	£400	
1906	924	6,910,128	£10	£30	£150	£300/
1907	925	5,947,895	£10	£30	£150	£300/
1908	926	3,280,010	£15	£40	£150	£270/
1909	927	3,482,289	£20	£120	£200	£420/
1910	928	5,650,713	£10	£25	£150	£250/

Victoria Veiled Head 1893 Florin

Edward VII 1902 Florin

GEORGE V .925 fine silver (until 1919) 28.5mm. Weight approx 11.3g.
The obverse is by Sir Bertram MacKennal (modified at various stages) and the first reverse design, based on the Jubilee Victoria issue is by an unknown designer, probably completed in house. From 1927 onwards the new reverse was designed by George Kruger Gray.

Date	ESC	Mintage	Fine	VF	EF	UNC/BU
1911	929	5,951,284	£6	£15	£25	£70/£80
1911	930	6,007 Proofs			£30	£70/£90
1912	931	8,571,731	£5	£15	£50	£100/
1913	932	4,545,278	£8	£20	£60	£150/
1914*	933	21,252,701	£4	£10	£25	£60/£70
1915	934	12,367,939	£4	£12	£25	£50/£60
1916	935	21,064,337	£4	£10	£30	£50/£60
1917	936	11,181,617	£5	£10	£35	£50/
1918	937	29,211,792	£4	£10	£35	£70/£90
1919	938	9,469,292	£5	£15	£30	£65/£100

George V 1911 Florin

GEORGE V .500 silver, 28.5mm

Date	ESC	Mintage	Fine	VF	EF	UNC/BU
1920*	939	15,387,833	£3	£9	£30	£65/£80
1921	940	34,863,895	£4	£8	£40	£65/£90
1922	941	23,861,044	£4	£6	£30	£55/£70
1923	942	21,546,533	£4	£6	£25	£50/£60
1923	ND	1 of BRITT points to tooth	GVF/NEF: £110			
1924	943	4,582,372	£4	£10	£40	£70/£90
1925	944	1,404,136	£10	£50	£200	£400/
1926	945	5,125,410	£3	£15	£50	£80/£90
1927	947	15,000 Proofs of new design				£65/£80
1928	948	11,087,186	£2	£4	£10	£25/£40
1929	949	16,397,279	£2	£4	£10	£25/£40
1930	950	5,753,568	£2	£4	£10	£28/£35
1931	951	6,556,331	£2	£4	£9	£28/£35
1932	952	717,041	£12	£50	£180	£360/£400
1933	953	8,685,303	£2	£4	£10	£16/£30
1935	954	7,540,546		£3	£6	£14/£25
1936	955	9,897,448		£2	£5	£14/£25

*1914 Large rim teeth or small rim teeth reported.

* 1920 'BRITT' has either 'I' pointing directly at, or between rim beads. Both varieties are rarely distinguished.

George V 1936
2nd Type Florin, 1927-36

EDWARD VIII .500 silver, 28.5mm. As George VI but with ER initials.
The planned reverse was the George VI type - with ER instead of GR - designed by George Kruger Gray. The obverse was by Thomas Humphrey Paget. This was not officially issued.

Date	ESC	Mintage	VF	EF	UNC/BU
1937	955A	3-4 Examples known.		Approx	£20,000/£30,000

GEORGE VI .500 silver (until 1946), 28.5mm. Weight 11.33g.
Thomas Humphey Paget designed the bust of George VI. The reverse was the work of George Kruger Gray.

Date	ESC	Mintage	VF	EF	UNC/BU
1937	956	13,006,781	£2	£3	£8/£10
1937	957	26,402 Proofs			£12/£18
1938	958	7,909,388	£3	£10	£25/£30
1939	959	20,850,607	£2	£4	£6/£8
1940	960	18,700,338	£2	£3	£10/£12
1941	961	24,451,079	£1	£3	£9/£11
1942	962	39,895,243	£1	£3	£5/£7
1943	963	26,711,987	£1	£3	£8/£10
1944	964	27,560,005	£1	£3	£4/£7
1945	965	25,858,049	£1	£2	£4/£6
1946	966	22,910,085	£1	£2	£4/£7

Now Cupro-Nickel (no silver), 28.5mm. Weight 11.3g.

Date	ESC	Mintage	VF	EF	UNC/BU
1947	967	22,910,085		£2	£5/£8
1948	968	67,553,636		£1	£5/£7
1949	968A	28,614,939		£2	£10/£12
1950	968B	24,357,490		£2	£10/£12
1950	968C	17,513 Proofs		FDC	£15
1951	968D	27,411,747		£3	£9/£11
1951	968E	20,000 Proofs		FDC	£12

George VI 1937 Florin.
IND:IMP was removed in 1949.

ELIZABETH II Cupro-Nickel (no silver), 28.5mm. Weight 11.5g
The bust was by Mary Gillick, the reverse was the work of Edgar Fuller, modelled by Cecil Thomas. As with the other denominations, the 1953 coins usually have poorly defined details on the head. The dies were improved for the 1954 issue onwards. In 1954 the title BRITT OMN was removed from the coins.

Date	ESC	Mintage	EF	UNC/BU
1953	968F	11,958,710	£1	£2/£4
1953	968G	40,000 Proofs		£10/£12
1954	968H	13,085,422	£5	£25/£35
1955	968I	25,887,253	£2	£5/£8
1956	968J	47,824,500	£2	£5/£8
1957	968K	33,071,282	£4	£25/£30
1958	968L	9,564,580	£2	£12/£20
1959	968M	14,080,319	£5	£15/£25
1960	968N	13,831,782	£1	£4/£6
1961	968O	37,735,315	£1	£4/£6
1962	968P	35,147,903	50p	£3/£5
1963	968Q	25,562,000	50p	£3/£5
1964	968R	16,539,000	50p	£2/£5
1965	968S	48,163,000	50p	£1/£3
1966	968T	84,041,000	50p	£1/£2
1967*	968U	39,718,000	50p	£1/£2
1967	ND	Double tails error	£75	£95/£125
1970	968V	Proofs 750,476 from set		£3/£4

*1967 Mintage figure includes over 17 million struck in 1968 but dated 1967

Eliabeth II 1965 Florin. The 1953 Florins
had BRITT:OMN in the obverse legend.

GEORGE III .925 fine silver, 32mm. Weight 14.1g
The last Half Crowns issued for circulation before 1817 were dated 1751 (George II), although Spanish coins were countermarked with the bust of George III to supply the demand until the re-coinage of 1816. Thomas Wyon junior (cousin of William Wyon) was responsible for the first head, which became known as the 'Bull' head. The King didn't like it, and it was changed in 1817 to a Pistucci version. Thomas Wyon designed the first half crown reverse, and the second was a modified version.

Date	ESC	Mintage	Fine	VF	EF	UNC/BU
1st 'Bull' style head						
1816	613		£18	£40	£160	£450/
1817	616	8,092,656	£15	£40	£175	£500/
1817	616A	'D' of 'DEI' over 'T'	£100	£250		
1817	ND	E of DEF over R&E	NEF	£400	Adams/Spink 2005	
1817	ND	S of PENSE over I	NEF	£260	Adams/Spink 2005	

2nd Type, with Re-designed smaller head and new reverse.

1817	618	Included above	£18	£35	£140	£450/
1817	618A	S's in Motto mirrored		Very Rare		
1818	621	2,905,056	£15	£35	£200	£450/
1819	623	4,790,016	£15	£35	£200	£450/
1819	ND	9 Struck over 8		£900	Adams/Spink 2005	
1819	ND	HO & SO over smaller ho & so	£240	Adams/Spink 2005		
1820	625	2,396,592 (Inc GIV)	£25	£70	£200	£400/

George III 1817 1st type
'Bull Head' Half Crown

George III 1818 2nd Type Half Crown

GEORGE IV .925 fine silver, 32mm. Weight 14.1g

Bennedetto Pistrucci designed the first Romanesque laureate head but refused to copy Sir Francis Chantrey's work, so the second bust was engraved by William Wyon. All three reverses were the work of Jean Baptiste Merlen. The first reverse type is shown on the front cover, and the second reverse type is very similar to the second shilling reverse. The third reverse is illustrated below.

Date	ESC	Mintage	Fine	VF	EF	UNC/BU
1st Roman style Laureate head.						
1820	628	Inc above, 1st Rev	£20	£50	£160	£350/
1821	631	1,435,104, 1st Rev	£20	£50	£160	£380/
1821*	ND	Heavier garnishing 1st Rev	£50	£130	£400	
1823	633	2,003,760 1st Rev	£500	£1000	£2500	
1823	634	Inc above, 2nd Rev	£20	£50	£160	£350/
1824	636	465,696 ?	£20	£90	£250	£450/£600
2nd Bare, thinner William Wyon head with 3rd reverse.						
1824	639	3-4 known, 3rd Rev	Expensive!			
1825	642	2,258,784	£24	£80	£275	£500/
1826	646	2,189,088	£28	£75	£200	£450/
1828	648	49,890 ?	£80	£200	£600	
1829	649	508,464	£35	£100	£400	

George IV 1st head

* 1821 - The reverse type with heavier shield garnishing also has the left leg of the A of ANNO pointing just to the right of a rim denticle. has heavier shield garnishing.

George IV 1825 Half Crown (2nd head)

William IV 1834 Half Crown

WILLIAM IV .925 fine silver, 32mm. Weight 14.1g
Jean Baptiste Merlen designed and engraved the reverse

Date	ESC	Mintage	Fine	VF	EF	UNC/BU
1831	656	5-10 examples	Expensive!			
1834	660	993,168 block WW	£80	£200	£600	£1000/
1834	662	WW script	£15	£60	£180	£300/
1835	665	281,952	£35	£100	£250	
1836	666	1,588,752	£20	£80	£200	£400/
1836	666A	6 over 5	£25	£100	£250	£450/
1837	667	150,526	£80	£150	£400	£700/

VICTORIA .925 fine silver, 32mm. Weight 14.1g
W Wyon designed and engraved the young head of Queen Victoria. In 1874 the design was modified and struck in lower relief. J B Merlen designed and engraved the reverse.

Date	ESC	Mintage	Fine	VF	EF	UNC/BU
Young Head:						
1839A	668		£250	£600	£1000	£2000/
1839B	671		£350	£750	£2000	£3000/
1839	672	WW incuse	£500	£1600	£4000	
1840	673	386,496	£90	£250	£550	
1841	674	42,768	£700	£1500	£3400	
1842	675	486,288	£40	£100	£450	
1843	676	454,608	£100	£300	£850	£1200/
1844	677	1,999,008	£50	£150	£400	£800/
1845	679	2,231,856	£40	£100	£300	£700/
1846	680	1,539,668	£60	£150	£400	£650/
1846	ND	8 over 6	£500	Adams/Spink 2005		
1848	681	Irregular obv lettering		£1300		
1848*	681A	367,488. 8/6		£1400		
1848	ND	8 over 7 £260 (DNW 2006)				
1849	682	261,360 large date		£100	£350	
1849	683	Small date	£100	£350	£900	
1849	ND	9 over 7 (or double struck 9) Fine: £150				
1850	684	484,613	£150	£350	£500	
1874	692	2,188,599	£30	£90	£180	£350/
1875	696	1,113,483	£40	£100	£200	£350/
1876	699	633,221	£30	£65	£170	£350/
1876	699A	6 over 5	£30	£60	£140	£350/
1877	700	447,059	£25	£60	£140	£350/
1878	701	1,466,232	£25	£70	£140	£350/
1879	703	901,356	£35	£100	£140	£350/
1880	705	1,346,350	£35	£60	£140	£300/
1881	707	2,301,495	£25	£60	£180	£320/
1882	710	808,227	£30	£100	£240	£450/
1883	711	2,982,779	£20	£65	£150	£300/
1884	712	1,569,175	£20	£65	£150	£300/
1885	713	1,628,438	£20	£65	£130	£300/
1886	715	891,767	£20	£65	£150	£300/
1887	717	261,747	£35	£140	£200	£350/

1839 - A: Queen has one plain, and one ornamented hair tie. B: Queen has two ornamental hair ties.

Victoria Young Head 1874 Half Crown

VICTORIA Jubilee head .925 fine silver, 32mm. Weight 14.1g
Sir Joseph Boehm designed the Jubilee head, which was engraved by Leonard Charles Wyon. Mr Wyon also engraved the reverse, from his own design. The old head bust was by Sir Thomas Brock, who was also responsible for the reverse design. Both sides of the old head half crown were engraved by George William de Saulles.

Date	ESC	Mintage	Fine	VF	EF	UNC/BU
1887	719	1,176,299	£5	£12	£25	£35/£40
1887	720	1,084 Proofs				£135/£175
1888	721	1,428,787	£8	£15	£30	£70/£100
1889	722	4,811,954	£8	£15	£40	£90/
1890	723	3,228,111	£8	£15	£40	£100/
1891	724	2,284,632	£10	£25	£80	£150/
1892	725	1,710,946	£9	£20	£80	£150/
Old, Veiled, or Widow Head type:						
1893	726	1,792,600	£6	£20	£40	£90/£120
1893	727	1,312 Proofs				£140/
1894	728	1,524,960	£8	£20	£100	£120/
1895	729	1,772,662	£12	£30	£80	£190/£250
1896	730	2,148,505	£10	£20	£60	£110/£200
1897	731	1,678,643	£10	£20	£80	£140/£190
1898	732	1,870,055	£10	£20	£50	£100/£150
1899	733	2,863,872	£10	£20	£50	£100/
1900	734	4,479,128	£10	£25	£60	£90/
1901	735	1,516,570	£10	£20	£50	£100/£140

Victoria Jubilee Head 1887 Half Crown

Victoria Veiled Head 1893 Half Crown

EDWARD VII .925 fine silver, 32mm. Weight 14.14g

Both obverse and reverse were the work of George William de Saulles.

Date	ESC	Mintage	Fine	VF	EF	UNC/BU
1902	746	1,316,008	£12	£30	£65	£90/£120
1902	747	15,123 Matt Proofs			£50	£80/£100
1903	748	274,840	£80	£450	£1200	
1904	749	709,652	£70	£200	£400	£1000/
1905	750	166,008	£300	£1000		
1906	751	2,886,206	£35	£60	£250	£400/
1907	752	3,693,930	£15	£60	£200	£350/
1908	753	1,758,889	£20	£60	£500	
1909	754	3,051,592	£25	£60	£350	£600/£750
1910	755	2,557,685	£12	£50	£150	£250/£350

GEORGE V .925 fine silver (until 1920), 32mm. Weight 14.14g

The obverse is by Sir Bertram MacKennal (which was modified at various stages) and the first reverse design is a slightly modified version of the Edward VII type. From 1927 onwards a different reverse was used, this was designed by George Kruger Gray.

Date	ESC	Mintage	Fine	VF	EF	UNC/BU
1911	757	2,914,573	£5	£20	£50	£110/£150
1911	758	6,007 Proofs				£90/£110
1912	759	4,700,789	£8	£20	£60	£150/
1913	760	1,090,160	£10	£25	£60	£150/
1914	761	18,333,003	£5	£14	£30	£70/£100
1915	762	32,433,066	£4	£6	£30	£70/£100
1916	763	29,530.020	£4	£8	£35	£70/
1917	764	11,172.052	£4	£10	£35	£80/£100
1918	765	29,079,592	£4	£10	£35	£80/£100
1919	766	10,266,737	£5	£10	£35	£80/£100

Edward VII 1909 Half Crown

George V 1917 Half Crown

GEORGE V Debased .500 silver, 32mm. Weight 14.14g:

Date	ESC	Mintage	Fine	VF	EF	UNC/BU
1920	767	17,983,077		£10	£40	£80/£100
1920	ND	Small head, high relief				
		Obv 1/Rev B (2001) BU £110				
1921	768	23,677,889		£6	£25	£50/£70
1922*	769	16,396,774 Rev A		£6	£30	£60/£70
	ND	Rev B		£9	£25	£40/£65
1923	770	26,308,526		£9	£25	£40/£70
1924	771	5,866,294		£6	£40	£70/£95
1925	772	1,413,461	£16	£70	£300	£460/
1926	773	4,473,516	£5	£30	£80	£180/
1926	773A	No colon after OMN		£25	£165	£260/
1926	774	Mod Effigy (Appendix I) £5		£20	£35	£100/
1927	775	6,852,872		£8	£20	£40/£50
1927	776	15,000 Proofs of New design				£40/£50
1928*	777	18,762,727		£8	£20	£45/£60
1929*	778	17,632,636		£4	£10	£35/£50
1930	779	809,501	£7	£80	£250	
1931	780	11,264,468		£5	£15	£40/£50
1932	781	4,793,643		£7	£15	£30/£50
1933	782	10,311,494		£3	£10	£20/£30
1934	783	2,422,399		£8	£30	£70/£90
1935	784	7,022,216		£3	£15	£30/£40
1936	785	7,039,423		£2	£9	£25/£40
1936	ND	Prooflike/Early strike				£70/

George V 1935 Half Crown reverse.
Used 1927-1936

EDWARD VIII, .500 silver, 32mm
The proposed reverse by George Kruger Gray featured a rectangular Royal standard flag. The obverse was by Thomas Humphrey Paget. This coin was never officially issued, and the reverse was not used again.

Date	ESC	Mintage	Fine	VF	EF	UNC/BU
1937	785A	Royal arms Flag reverse. Approx				£28,000

George VI 1945 Half Crown

GEORGE VI .500 silver (until 1946), 32mm. Weight 14.14g
Thomas Humphey Paget designed the bust of George VI. The reverse was the work of George Kruger Gray.

Date	ESC	Mintage	Fine	VF	EF	UNC/BU
1937	786	9,106,440	50p	£1	£4	£12/£20
1937	787	26,402 Proofs			FDC	£25
1938	788	6,426,478	50p	£1	£9	£20/£30
1939	789	15,478,635	50p	£1	£5	£10/£14
1940	790	17,948,439	50p	£1	£3	£8/£10
1941	791	15,773,984	50p	£1	£3	£8/£10
1942	792	31,220,090	50p	£1	£3	£8/£10
1942	ND	Specimen strike (also of 1943)			£80/	
1943	793	15.462,875	50p	£1	£3	£9/£12
1944	794	15,255,165	50p	£1	£3	£9/£12
1945	795	19,849,242	50p	£1	£3	£5/£8
1946	796	22,724,873	50p	£1	£3	£5/£8

Cupro-Nickel (No Silver), 32mm. Weight 14.22g:

Date	ESC	Mintage	EF	UNC/BU
1947	797	21,911,484	£2	£5/£7
1948	798	71,164,703	£2	£4/£6

IND: IMP legend (Emperor of India) discontinued.

Date	ESC	Mintage	EF	UNC/BU
1949	798A	28,272,512	£3	£8/£11
1950	798B	28,335,500	£2	£15/£20
1950	798C	17,513 Proofs	FDC	£12
1951	798D	9,003,520	£3	£15/£20
1951	798E	20,000 Proofs	FDC	£20
1952	798F	1 or 2 Known	Approx	£30,000

ELIZABETH II Cupro-Nickel (No Silver), 32mm. Weight 14.2g
Mary Gillick designed the first bust of Elizabeth II. The reverse was
the work of Edgar Fuller, modeled by Cecil Thomas.

Date	ESC	Mintage	EF	UNC/BU
1953	798G	4,333,214 Obv 1	£1	£3/£5
1953	ND	Obv 2	£2	£4/£6
1953	798H	40,000 Proofs	FDC	£20
1954	798I	11,614,953	£10	£40/£50
1955	798J	23,628,726	£1	£9/£13
1956	798K	33,934,909	£2	£14/£25
1957	798L	34,200,563	£2	£7/£9
1958	798M	15,745,668	£3	£22/£30
1959	798N	9,028,844	£4	£15/£25
1960	798O	19,929,191		£7/£10
1961	798P	25,887,89		£3/£5
1962	798S	24,013,312		£2/£4
1963	798T	17,557,600		£2/£4
1964	798U	5,973,600		£2/£4
1965	798V	9,878,400		£1/£3
1966	798W	13,384,000		70p/£2
1967	798X	33,058,400		60/£1
1970	798Y	Proofs from the set		£5/£8

Elizabeth II 1966 Half Crown

Bank of England Tokens

GEORGE III .925 fine silver, 34-35mm. Accurate weight not known at time of writing.
Another short token issue, struck under the authority of the Bank of England in order to provide much needed change until the major re-coinage of 1816. Two bust types were used on these during their short run. The first bust is the military type as shown below, the second bust was a not entirely attractive laureate head type. There are five non proof varieties of 1811, and six different proof types! The die varieties can be spotted using: on the obverse, the front leaf of the laurel and its relationship with the 'E' of 'DEI', and on the reverse, the number of acorns in the oak wreath:

Type 1 = Obv: front leaf points to end of 'E'. Rev: has 27 acorns present.
Type 2 = Obv: front leaf points to end of 'E'. Rev: has 26 acorns present.
Type 3 = Obv: front leaf points to gap between 'D' and 'E'. Rev: has 26 acorns present.
Type 4 = Obv: front leaf points to gap between 'D' and 'E'. Rev: has 25 acorns present.
Type 5 = Obv: front leaf points to the upright of 'E'. Rev: has 24 acorns present.

Date	ESC	Mintage or Details	Fine	VF	EF	UNC/BU
1811	407	Type 1(Scarce)	£20	£60	£120	
1811	408	Type 2(Commonest)	£17	£45	£100	
1811	410	Type 3(Rarer)		£70	£100	£150
1811	411	Type 4(Rarer)		£70	£100	£150
1811	413	Type 5(Rarer)		£70	£100	£150
1812	415	(1st head)	£17	£70	£100	£200/
1812	416	(2nd head)	£17	£70	£120	£200/
1813	421		£17	£70	£100	£150/
1814	422		£17	£70	£100	£150/
1815	423		£17	£70	£100	£150/
1816	424		£100	£500		

George III Three Shilling Bank Token. On
the obverse, the front leaf of the laurel
points to the gap between the 'D' and 'E'.

VICTORIA .925 fine silver, 36mm. Weight 22.62g
Sir Joseph Boehm designed the Jubilee head, which was engraved by Leonard Charles Wyon. Mr Wyon also engraved the reverse, from his own design. The denomination was not popular, as it was often confused for a crown and became known as the 'barmaids ruin'.

Date	ESC	Mintage or Details	Fine	VF	EF	UNC/BU
1887	394	483,347 Roman I	£9	£20	£50	£80/£90
1887	395	Arabic 1 in date	£10	£18	£35	£90/£100
1888	397	243,340	£20	£40	£90	£140/
1888*	397A	Inverted 1 VICTORIA	£20	£45	£150	£300/
1889	398	1,185,111	£12	£25	£100	£150/
1889*	398A	Inverted 1 VICTORA	£20	£45	£130	£220/
1890	399	782,146	£12	£25	£100	£150/

* The second 'I' in 'VICTORIA' appears to be an upside-down 'I'. It is in fact a damaged 'I'.

Queen Victoria Jubilee Head 1887
Double Florin with Arabic '1'.

There are also 2 slightly different obverse types noted for
the 'Arabic' 1887 coin. The easiest way to spot them con-
cerns the 'D' of 'DEI' and exactly to which bead in the Crown
it is level with. Both types are believed common.

Bank of England Five Shilling token

GEORGE III .925 fine silver, 41mm. Accurate weight not known at time of writing. The largest denomination of the Bank of England token issues. The Dollar started life with a face value of five shillings, but did rise to five shillings and sixpence for six years while silver was in short supply. All are dated 1804, although they were struck up to 1811 and remained legal tender until 1820, by which time their face value was back to five shillings. There are seventeen proof varieties of this coin in various metals, and ten non proof varieties, as a result of slightly different obverse and reverse die combinations being used. They were struck on Spanish/Spanish colonial Pieces of Eight and coins with lots of Spanish detail, especially dates and mintmarks do attract a premium. A picture of an 1804 Dollar can be seen on the previous page.

Type 1 = Obv: front leaf points to upright of 'E'. Rev: raised 'K' under shield.
Type 2 = Obv: front leaf points to upright of 'E'. Rev: inverted incuse ' Ж '.
Type 3 = Obv: as above, but no stops between CHK on neck. Rev: raised 'K' under shield.
Type 4 = Obv: as 1 but leaf points to centre of 'E'. Rev: raised 'K' under shield.
Type 5 = Obv: as 1 but leaf points to centre of 'E'. Rev: inverted raised ' Ж '
Type 6 = Obv: as 1 but leaf points to centre of 'E'. Rev: inverted incuse ' Ж '.
Type 7 = Obv: as 1 but leaf points to right end of 'E'. Rev: raised 'K' under shield.
Type 8 = Obv: as 1 but leaf points to right end of 'E'. Rev: inverted raised ' Ж '
Type 9 = Obv: as 1 but leaf points to right end of 'E'. Rev: inverted incuse ' Ж '.
Type 10 = Obv: no stop after REX, leaf to centre of 'E'. Rev: raised 'K' under shield.

Date	ESC	Type	Fine	VF	EF
1804	144	Type 1 (commonest)	£100	£140	£300
1804	147	Type 2 (very rare)	£160	£300	
1804	148	Type 3 (rare)	£130	£250	£320
1804	149	Type 4 (scarce)	£120	£250	
1804	153	Type 5 (rare)	£130	£275	
1804	156	Type 6 (scarce)	£125	£300	
1804	158	Type 7 (ext. rare)	£200	£450	
1804	159	Type 8 (very rare)	£150	£300	
1804	162	Type 9 (very rare)	£150	£300	
1804	164	Type 10 (common)	£130	£200	

George III Dollar Bank Token. On the obverse, the front leaf points to the upright of the 'E'.

GEORGE III .925 fine silver, 37.6mm. Weight 28.2759g
Dies designed and engraved by Benedetto Pistrucci. This was the first time a St George and the Dragon design had been used since the reign of Henry VIII.

Date	Edge	ESC	Mintage	Fine	VF	EF	UNC/BU
1818	LVIII	211	155,232	£20	£75	£250	£400/£500
1818*	LVIII	213A	Error edge	£700	£1800	£3750	
1818	LIX	214	Inc above	£20	£75	£250	£400/£500
1819	LIX	215	683,496	£20	£75	£275	£400/£500
1819	LIX	215A	No stops on edge		£100	£375	£500/£750
1819	LIX	215B	9 over 8	£100	£200	£500	
1819	LX	216	Inc above	£20	£80	£200	£350/£500
1819*	LX	ND	TVTAMEN	£60	£150	£400	
1820	LX	219	448,272	£20	£75	£250	£350/£500
1820	LX	220A	20 over 19	£100	£250		
1820	LX	ND	S over T (Soit)	£150	£360		

* 1818 Error edge reads: DECVS ANNO REGNI ET TVTAMEN.
* 1819 No stop after the word TVTAMEN.

George III 1818 Crown

George IV 1821 Crown

GEORGE IV .925 fine silver, Laureate Roman style head 37.6mm. Weight 28.2759g
The obverse and reverse were designed by Benedetto Pistrucci and engraved by Jean Baptiste Merlen.

Date	Edge	ESC	Mintage	Fine	VF	EF	UNC/BU
1821	SEC*	246	437,976	£35	£280	£600	£900/
1822	SEC*	251	124,929	£35	£200	£650	£1000/
1822	TER*	252	Inc Above	£35	£180	£600	£1000/

* SEC = SECUNDO, TER= TERTIO - Regnal year on the edge.

WILLIAM IV .925 fine silver, 38mm
No William IV Crowns were issued for general circulation.

VICTORIA .925 fine silver Young Head, 38mm. Weight approx 28.35g
William Wyon produced the Young head Victoria portrait. The reverse was the work of Jean Baptiste Merlen, before his retirement in 1844. The gothic portrait on the later gothic crowns (not included in this section) were the work of William Wyon. The reverse of the gothic crown is by William Dyce.

Date	Edge	ESC	Mintage	Fine	VF	EF	UNC/BU
1844	VIII	280	94,248 Star stops	£30	£120	£400	£1000/
1844	VIII	281	Cinquefoil stops*	£30	£120	£400	£900/
1845	VIII	282A	159,192 Star stops	£30	£120	£400	£1000/
1845	VIII	ND	Star stops, error edge, reads: AANNO	£500			
1845	VIII	282	Cinquefoil stops*	£30	£120	£400	£1000/
1847	XI	286	140,976	£100	£700	£1600	

Gothic Crowns were not intended for circulation, and are therefore listed in the proof section.
* A cinquefoil is a pattern of five leaves.

Victoria Young Head 1845 Crown

VICTORIA .925 fine silver Jubilee Head, 38.6mm.. Weight approx 28.35g
Sir Joseph Boehm designed the Jubilee head, which was engraved by Leonard Charles Wyon. The reverse on both
the jubilee head crown and the old head crown is the classic Benedetto Pistrucci St George slaying the dragon
design. The old head bust was by Sir Thomas Brock. A regnal edge year was used on the old head crown, and
because Victoria was not crowned on January 1st, this results in two different regnal year types for each date.

Date	ESC	Mintage	Fine	VF	EF	UNC/BU
887	296	173,581	£12	£22	£50	£100/£140
887	297	1,084 Proofs			£200	£300/£400
888	298	131,899 Close date	£12	£35	£85	£180/ £220
888	ND	Wide date	£30	£90	£250	£350/
889	299	1,807,223	£12	£25	£65	£100/£120
890	300	997,862	£18	£38	£100	£200/
891	301	566,394	£14	£25	£90	£190/£250
892	302	451,334	£20	£45	£125	£250/

Victoria 1887 Jubilee Head Crown

VICTORIA .925 fine silver Old, Veiled or Widow Head, 38.6mm.. Weight approx 28.35g

Date	Edge	ESC	Mintage	Fine	VF	EF	UNC/BU
1893	LVI	303	497,845	£14	£30	£120	£250/
1893	LVI	304	1,312 Proofs			£120	£260/
1893	LVII	305	Inc Above	£30	£65	£200	£250/
1894	LVII	306	144,906	£12	£40	£150	£260/
1894	LVIII	307	Inc Above	£15	£40	£150	£280/
1895	LVII	308	252,862	£15	£40	£150	£250/
1895	LIX	309	Inc Above	£12	£45	£150	£180/
1896	LIX	310	317,599	£12	£40	£150	£250/
1896	LX	311	Inc Above	£12	£40	£150	£250/
1897	LX	312	262,118	£11	£40	£100	£220/
1897	LXI	313	Inc Above	£12	£40	£100	£220/
1898	LXI	314	161,450	£20	£100	£200	£350/
1898	LXII	315	Inc Above	£15	£40	£100	£240/
1899	LXII	316	166,300	£15	£40	£120	£240/
1899	LXIII	317	Inc Above	£12	£40	£140	£270/
1900	LXIII	318	353,356	£20	£55	£150	£300/
1900	LXIV	319	Inc Above	£20	£60	£150	£300/

Queen Victoria Veiled Head 1893 Crown

Edward VII 1902 Crown. (Reverse type was the same as the Veiled Head Victorian crowns)

EDWARD VII .925 fine silver, 38.6mm.. Weight approx 28.35g

A one year only issue, and the very last British crown made for circulation (the latter ones being commemorative/special issues only). The bust is by George William de Saulles, and the reverse is the St George type by Benedetto Pistrucci.

Date	Edge	ESC	Mintage	Fine	VF	EF	UNC/BU
1902	II	361	256,020	£20	£60	£80	£180/
1902	II	362	15,123 Matt Proofs			£60	£130/

GEORGE V .500 silver, 38.6mm. Weight approx 28.4g

In 1927 the mint decided to produce proof sets of the newly designed coinage. The crown, among other coins, was produced as a proof striking only, to be sold in these sets. The design was popular, so subsequently a small number of crowns were struck annually, mainly to provide the public with keepsakes, which were often given as gifts at Christmas time. The popular 'Wreath' crown was produced annually (except 1935) until the death of the king in 1936. In 1935 to celebrate the kings' Silver Jubilee a larger number of special crowns were struck featuring an Art Deco St George slaying the dragon. The bust on both coins was the standard Bertram MacKennal design. The wreath reverse was by George Kruger Gray, and the jubilee crown reverse was by Percy Metcalfe. Many have critisized the Art Deco St George, but personally I think it looks classically 30s, and makes a nice change from the Pistrucci version. The king himself had mixed feelings, saying that St George looked 'A damned bad rider'. The design was approved, so he couldn't have entirely hated it!

Date	Edge	ESC	Mintage	Fine	VF	EF	UNC/BU
1927		367	15,030 Proofs			£100	£150/£250
1928		368	9,034		£100	£150	£300/
1929		369	4,994		£110	£200	£300/£400
1930		370	4,847	£100	£150	£300	£400/
1931		371	4,056		£150	£240	£350/
1932		372	2,395	£200	£400	£500	£600/
1933		373	7,132		£130	£230	£350/
1934		374	932	£1500	£1900	£2400	£3400/£4200
1935*		375	714,769 incuse edge		£5	£15	£20/£30
1935*		375A	Error edge lettering**		£900		
1935*		376	SPECIMEN striking, in original box				£40/£50
1936		381	2,473	£200	£280	£500	£600/

* The 1935 coins all feature the George slaying the dragon reverse, not the wreath type reverse.
**The non proof 1935 error edge has a large space after 'ANNO' and some missing letters.

Left to right - The first two images are the obverse and reverse of a
1928 Wreath Crown. The last image is the reverse of the 1935 Crown.
The 1935 Crown obverse was similar to the Wreath Crown.

EDWARD VIII .500 silver, 38.6mm

Date	ESC	Mintage	VF	EF	UNC/BU
1937	391C	Reverse as George VI 1937. Approximately			£75,000

GEORGE VI .500 silver, 38.6mm . Weight approx 28.2g
The bust for all George VI coins was by Thomas Humphrey Paget. The reverse of the coronation coin was by George Kruger Gray. The reverse of the 1951 Festival of Britain coin was created by re-using an 1899 crown die with a manually adjusted date. The Festival of Britain crown boxes exist as either matchbox/slide open style, or as boxes with a lift off lid. Coins in green boxes are a little less common.

Date	ESC	Mintage	VF	EF	UNC/BU
1937	392	418,699 Coronation	£9	£13	£22/£30
1937	393	26,402 Proofs from the sets			£30/£40

Cupro-Nickel (No silver), 38.6mm. Struck for the Festival of Britain in 1951.

Date	ESC	Mintage	VF	EF	UNC/BU
1951	393C	1,983,540 Highly prooflike		£4	£6/£10
1951		In box of issue, green or purple		£6	£10/£18
1951	ND	Error edge lettering - Blundered latin date and large space			
		before 'FLORET' [Predecimal.com 2006]			£300/

The reverse of the 1937 Crown (obv is similar to the 1951 Crown, but with 'FIVE SHILLINGS' under the bust).

1951 Crown - The reverse used for these was a re-cycled 1899 Crown die with the date amended by hand

Queen Elizabeth II 1953 Crown

ELIZABETH II Cupro-Nickel (No silver), 38.6mm . Weight 28.2g (28.4g 1965)
The coronation crown was an interesting departure from tradition, featuring the monarch on horseback; the first time this had been done since the reign of Charles I. Gilbert Ledward designed the obverse and the reverse was a joint effort by Edgar Fuller and Cecil Thomas. The edge has the words 'FAITH AND TRUTH I WILL BEAR UNTO YOU'. The New York Trades fair and Churchill crowns have the young bust by Mary Gillick. The Trades Fair crown uses the same reverse as the coronation crown. The reverse of the Churchill crown was modelled from a bust by Croatian artist Oscar Nemon. The actual bust, which is now part of the Government Art Collection looks much nicer than the quite low relief design on the much criticized crown.

Date	ESC	Mintage	VF	EF	UNC/BU
1953	393F	5,962,621		£3	£4/£6
1953	393G	40,000 Proofs		£15	£20/£30
1953	ND	(Hip Hop) Edge Error:"...WILL BEAR UNTO YO"(no 'U')			
			£30	£40	£60/£80
1960	393K	1,024,038 British Trades Fair issue	£4	£6/£8	
1960	393L	70,000 Polished die specials in box	£5	£12/£20	
1965	393N	19,640,000 Churchill issue	25p	75p/£1	

From left to right: The obverse of the 1960 Crown (Reverse type was as the 1953 Crown). Obv and Rev of the 1965 Churchill Crown.

Gold Section: Sovereign based denominations 1817 - 1968

An act of parliament was implemented on the 3rd August 1816, stating that new gold coins were to be minted to replace the Guinea and its fractions. The new sovereigns were given a face value of 20 shillings (One pound Sterling) and the half sovereigns were logically worth 10 shillings. The new coins were all struck using machinery installed at the new Tower Hill site, which until a few years previous, had been occupied by tobacco warehouses.

The sovereign, being a new denomination and smaller (the sovereign is about 22mm, the half sovereign 19.5mm) than the established guinea, was not popular at first. The government stuck with it and popularity soon grew. 191 years later, the sovereign is one of the most popular gold coins in the world!

Benedetto Pistrucci came up with idea of having a Saint George motif on the reverse. At that time his artistic reputation had gained him quite a celebrity status and he was commissioned to design the Saint George and the bust of King George III for use on the new coins. As if that wasn't enough, he was also given the task of engraving the dies for the coins too.

Gold, being quite inert, tends to stay bright and for that reason the BU grade is not shown. Gold is heavy too and quite soft, so is more prone to being marked and scratched. Problems with the eye appeal will of course affect the value. At the time of writing (Mid September 2008) the price of gold bullion is historically pretty high. A sovereign is worth £110.00 for its gold content (half that for a half sovereign). Gold prices fluctuate of course, so the internet or a newspaper should be checked for the current rate.

Specifications: All full sovereigns weigh 7.98 grammes and have a diameter of 22.05mm. Half sovereigns weigh 3.99 grammes and have a diameter of 19.5mm. The alloy used for both coins is 916.66 parts per 1000 pure gold (22 carat) which means that the gold content of an unworn and undamaged sovereign is 7.315 grammes and 3.658 grammes for a half sovereign.

George III 1820 Half Sovereign

George III

Date	Notes	F	VF	EF	UNC
1817		£120	£200	£350	£550
1818	2nd 8 over 7		£280	£600	£1500
1818		£140	£220	£380	£600
1820	Varieties exist	£110	£220	£380	£600

Rare proofs of 1817 and 1818 exist.

George IV Laureate Head

Date	Notes	F	VF	EF	UNC
1821	1st Reverse	£450	£1200	£2300	
1821	Proof	Rare			
1823	2nd Reverse	£150	£240	£450	£750
1824		£150	£240	£450	£700
1825		£150	£250	£400	£650

Bare head type from here down.

1826		£100	£200	£400	£700
1826	*	£90	£170	£350	£650
1826	Proof	Rare			
1827		£100	£200	£500	£700
1827	*	£90	£170	£450	£650
1828		£100	£200	£400	£720
1828	*	£95	£180	£420	£700

* Coins marked with an asterix were struck using a different obverse die. The border is heavier and an extra tuft of hair can be seen behind the Kings ear.

William IV

Date	Notes	F	VF	EF	UNC
1831	Plain edge proof	Rare			
1831	Milled edge proof	Rare			
1834		£150	£300	£740	£1250
1835		£170	£320	£640	£1000
1836		£200	£350	£725	£1100
1836	Error, struck using sixpence obv	Rare			
1837		£160	£320	£680	£1100

Victoria - Young Head
Commencing in this reign, gold coins were also minted at colonial mints in Australia, Canada and India. These colonial coins were given mintmarks to distinguish them, whereas London mint coins have no mintmark. The mintmarks used were capital letters. The letters and their positions will be pointed out in the listings. The mint letters and the various slightly different young head busts make this a difficult series to fully understand.

London mint coins with no mintmarks:

Date	Notes	F	VF	EF	UNC
1838		£100	£170	£400	£750
1839	Proof, plain or milled edge	Rare			
1841		£100	£170	£400	£725
1842		£80	£150	£300	£575
1843		£100	£170	£400	£680
1844		£90	£140	£300	£650
1845		£200	£430	£1350	
1846		£90	£150	£350	£650
1847		£90	£150	£350	£650
1848	Tight date	£90	£150	£350	£650
1848	2nd 8 over 7	£170	£300	£500	
1848	Loose date	£120	£180	£400	
1849		£85	£140	£300	£550
1850		£170	£330	£1200	
1851		£80	£130	£300	£550
1852		£90	£140	£300	£560
1853		£80	£120	£300	£550
1853	Proof, large or small dates	Rare			
1855		£80	£120	£300	£550
1856		£80	£120	£300	£550
1856	6 over	£130	£180	£350	£660
1857		£80	£130	£300	£560
1858		£80	£130	£300	£560
1858	Larger 2nd head type	£80	£140	£250	£450
1859		£80	£130	£250	£450
1860		£80	£130	£250	£450
1861		£80	£130	£250	£450
1862		£400	£1500	£4100	
1863		£80	£130	£250	£450

Now with die numbers below the shield

Date	Notes	F	VF	EF	UNC
1863		£85	£130	£340	£600
1864		£75	£120	£250	£440
1865		£75	£120	£250	£440
1866		£80	£130	£250	£440
1867		£80	£130	£250	£440
1869		£85	£140	£250	£440
1870		£60	£120	£250	£440
1870	With re-touched shield legend, coarser teeth.	£120	£300	£800	
1871		£80	£130	£250	£440
1871	With re-touched shield legend, coarser teeth.	£130	£300	£800	
1871	No die number	£220	£450		
1871	Queens' nose points to 'T'	£160	£300	£900	
1872	Queens' nose points to 'T'	£140	£260	£800	

Victoria 1866 Young head Half Sovereign

Half Sovereign (continued)

Date	Notes	F	VF	EF	UNC
1872	Larger head	£70	£100	£250	£440
1873		£70	£100	£250	£440
1874		£70	£100	£250	£440
1875		£70	£100	£250	£440
1876		£70	£100	£250	£440
1876	Narrow hair ribbon £65	£130	£280	£460	
1877		£70	£120	£250	£440
1878	Narrow hair ribbon £65	£130	£280	£460	
1879		£90	£150	£360	£700
1880		£75	£120	£280	£500

No die numbers from this point onwards.

Date	Notes	F	VF	EF	UNC
1880		£70	£120	£250	£440
1883		£70	£120	£250	£440
1884		£70	£120	£250	£440
1885		£70	£120	£250	£440
1885	5 over 3	£130	£200	£350	£730

Sydney mint coins, indicated here by an 'S' after the date and distinguished on the coin by a small 'S' under the shield.

Date	Notes	F	VF	EF	UNC
1871S		£70	£150	£700	£2500
1872S		£70	£150	£700	£2500
1875S		£70	£150	£700	£2500
1879S		£70	£150	£650	£2300
1880S		£70	£150	£650	£2300
1881S		£70	£150	£650	£2300
1882S		£170	£520	£2800	£7000
1882S	Legend close to heavy border (values approximately as above)				
1883S		£80	£140	£540	£3200
1883S	Legend close to heavy border (values approximately as above)				
1886S		£70	£140	£750	£2500
1887S		£70	£140	£750	£2500

Melbourne mint coins, indicated here by an 'M' after the date and distinguished on the coin by a small 'M' under the shield.

Date	Notes	F	VF	EF	UNC
1873M		£70	£140	£680	£2500
1877M		£70	£140	£680	£2500
1877M	Narrow hair ribbon	(values approximately as above)			
1881M		£100	£300	£1350	£4000
1882M	Narrow hair ribbon	£70	£130	£550	£1700
1882M		£70	£140	£550	£1750
1884M		£80	£250	£1450	£4000
1885M		£170	£380	£2000	£5400
1886M		£100	£200	£1500	£3800
1887M		£140	£500	£1900	£5400

Victoria - Jubilee Head

London Mint Coins.

Date	Notes	F	VF	EF	UNC
1887	JEB on truncation	BV	BV	£80	£110
1887	Small close JEB	BV	£80	£150	£250
1887	no JEB	BV	£80	£150	£250
1890	JEB on truncation	£85	£160	£250	
1890	no JEB	BV	BV	£80	£130
1890	*	BV	BV	£80	£130
1891		BV	£80	£150	£250
1891	*	BV	BV	£100	£140
1892	JEB on truncation	£80	£160	£250	
1892	no JEB	BV	£80	£160	£250
1892	*	BV	BV	£80	£130
1893	*	BV	£70	£110	£160

Victoria 1887 Jubilee head Half Sovereign

* Coins marked with an asterix have a lower
shield and a slightly spread apart date.

Sydney mint coins, indicated here by an 'S' after the date and distinguished
on the coin by a small 'S' under the shield.

1887S	Wide spaced JEB	£70	£160	£280	£900
1887S	Normal JEB	£70	£160	£280	£900
1889S		£80	£170	£500	£1800
1891S		£80	£170	£500	£1800
1891S	no JEB	£80	£170	£500	£1800

Melbourne mint coins, indicated here by an 'M' after the date and
distinguished on the coin by a small 'M' under the shield.

1887M	Wide spaced JEB	£70	£150	£280	£900
1887M	Close JEB	£70	£150	£280	£900
1893M		£70	£120	£400	£1500

Victoria - Veiled Head

The Pistrucci St George is back for now, and remains in constant use on half sovereigns right up to the present day. London mint coins are dealt with first.

Date	Notes	F	VF	EF	UNC
1893		BV	BV	£70	£120
1893	Proof				£500
1894		BV	BV	£70	£120
1895		BV	BV	£70	£120
1896		BV	BV	£70	£120
1897		BV	BV	£70	£120
1898		BV	BV	£70	£120
1899		BV	BV	£70	£120
1900		BV	BV	£70	£120
1901		BV	BV	£70	£120

Victoria 1896 Veiled head Half Sovereign

Melbourne mint coins, indicated here by an 'M' after the date and distinguished on the coin by a small 'M' on the gound below the horses right rear hoof.

Date	Notes	F	VF	EF	UNC
1893M		Rare			
1896M		£70	£120	£350	£1500
1899M		£70	£120	£350	£1500
1900M		£70	£120	£350	£1500

Perth mint coins, indicated here by a 'P' after the date and distinguished on the coin by a small 'P' on the gound below the horses right rear hoof.

Date	Notes	F	VF	EF	UNC
1899P	Proof		Unique		
1900P		£100	£170	£450	£2000

Sydney mint coins, indicated here by an 'S' after the date and distinguished on the coin by a small 'S' on the gound below the horses right rear hoof.

Date	Notes	F	VF	EF	UNC
1893S		£70	£120	£280	£1100
1897S		£70	£120	£250	£1000
1900S		£70	£100	£240	£1000

Edward VII

London mint coins listed first.

Date	Notes	F	VF	EF	UNC
1902		BV	BV	£70	£100
1902	Matte Proof				£135
1903		BV	BV	£65	£90
1904		BV	BV	£65	£90
1904	No B.P. in exergue BV	BV	£65	£100	
1905		BV	BV	£65	£90
1906		BV	BV	£65	£90
1907		BV	BV	£65	£90
1908		BV	BV	£65	£90
1909		BV	BV	£65	£90
1910		BV	BV	£65	£90

Edward VII 1909 Half Sovereign

Melbourne mint coins, indicated here by an 'M' after the date and distinguished on the coin by a small 'M' on the gound below the horses right rear hoof.

Date	Notes	F	VF	EF	UNC
1906M		£70	£120	£380	£1400
1907M		£65	£80	£100	£400
1908M		£65	£80	£120	£400
1909M		£65	£80	£120	£450

Perth mint coins, indicated here by a 'P' after the date and distinguished on the coin by a small 'P' on the gound below the horses right rear hoof.

Date	Notes	F	VF	EF	UNC
1904P	No B.P. in exergue £75	£200	£600	£1300	
1904P		£80	£180	£600	£1300
1908P		£80	£180	£600	£1300
1909P		£80	£180	£500	£1300

Sydney mint coins, indicated here by an 'S' after the date and distinguished on the coin by a small 'S' on the gound below the horses right rear hoof.

Date	Notes	F	VF	EF	UNC
1902S		BV	£70	£150	£380
1902S	Proof		Rare		
1903S		BV	£75	£180	£250
1906S		BV	£70	£180	£250
1908S		BV	£70	£90	£180
1910S		BV	£70	£90	£180

George V, London mint coins listed first

Date	Notes	F	VF	EF	UNC
1911		BV	BV	£60	£80
1911	Proof				£250
1911	Matte proof	Rare			
1912		BV	BV	£60	£80
1913		BV	BV	£60	£80
1914		BV	BV	£60	£80
1915		BV	BV	£60	£80

George V 1912 Half Sovereign

Melbourne mint coins, indicated here by an 'M' after the date and distinguished on the coin by a small 'M' on the gound below the horses right rear hoof.

Date	Notes	F	VF	EF	UNC
1915M		BV	BV	£65	£100

Perth mint coins, indicated here by a 'P' after the date and distinguished on the coin by a small 'P' on the gound below the horses right rear hoof.

Date	Notes	F	VF	EF	UNC
1911P		BV	£75	£120	£700
1915P		BV	£75	£100	£700
1918P		£150	£300	£550	£900

Sydney mint coins, indicated here by an 'S' after the date and distinguished on the coin by a small 'S' on the gound below the horses right rear hoof.

Date	Notes	F	VF	EF	UNC
1911S		BV	£65	£85	£120
1912S		BV	£65	£85	£100
1914S		BV	BV	£65	£80
1915S		BV	BV	£65	£80
1916S		BV	BV	£65	£80

Pretoria (South Africa) mint coins, indicated here by an 'SA' after the date and distinguished on the coin by a small 'SA' on the gound below the horses right rear hoof.

Date	Notes	F	VF	EF	UNC
1923SA	Proof				£300
1925SA		BV	BV	£65	£80
1926SA		BV	BV	£65	£80

Edward VII

Extremely rare, not to be confused with modern fantasy patterns.

George VI

This issue was a plain edged proof only, struck in London. 5001 were struck, the odd '1' was for the King himself.

1937	Plain edge Proof				£400

Elizabeth II - No half sovereigns issued until 1980.

George III

Date		F	VF	EF	UNC
1817		£250	£400	£800	£1200
1818		£350	£700	£1250	£2000
1818	Slanted colon after BRITANNIAR (values approx. as above)				
1818	Wiry curls, normal legend			Rare	
1818	Wiry curls, slanted colon as above			Rare	
1819					£75,000
1820		£250	£400	£800	£1250

George III 1820 Sovereign

Rare proofs exist of 1817, 1818 and 1820. Varieties of the
1820 coin also exist.

George IV

Date		F	VF	EF	UNC
1821		£225	£375	£750	£1250
1822		£300	£450	£900	£1500
1823		£450	£1250	£3500	
1824		£350	£500	£900	£1500
1825		£500	£1500	£3500	

George IV Laureate head 1821 Sovereign

Now using the bare head

		F	VF	EF	UNC
1825		£200	£400	£800	£1350
1826		£200	£400	£800	£1350
1827		£275	£450	£900	£1500
1828		£3000	£7500		
1829		£275	£450	£900	£1600
1830		£275	£450	£900	£1600

George IV Bare head 1830 Sovereign

Rare proofs exist of 1821, 1825 and 1826.

William IV

Date		F	VF	EF	UNC
1831		£300	£600	£1500	£2500
1831	WW incuse, no stops (values approximately double those shown above)				
1831	Nose points to 2nd I in BRITANNIAR Rare				
1832		£300	£500	£1250	£1750
1832	Nose points to 2nd I in BRITANNIAR (values approx same as above)				
1833		£300	£600	£1500	£2500
1835		£300	£600	£1500	£2500
1836		£300	£550	£1350	£2000
1836	N of ANNO in shield		Rare		
1837		£300	£550	£1350	£2000
1837	3 over 8	£400	£900	£1650	

William IV 1831 Sovereign

Rare proofs exist of 1830, 1831 and 1832.

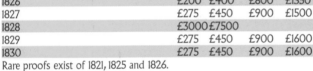

Victoria
The first coins listed here are all the shield reverse type, from the London mint.
Rare proofs exist for 1838 and 1839.

Date	Notes	F	VF	EF	UNC
1838		£250	£600	£1250	£2500
1839		£900	£1500	£3000	£6000
1841		£2000	£3500	£7500	£15000
1842		£150	£200	£400	£800
1842	Open 2	£200	£350	£700	£1400
1843		£150	£200	£400	£800
1843	2nd 3 over 2	£300	£750	£1500	£3000
1844	Large 44	£150	£200	£400	£800
1844	Smaller 44	£200	£300	£800	£1400
1844	date over inverted 4	Rare			
1845		£150	£200	£400	£800
1845	date over inverted 4	Rare			
1845	1 for 1 in date	£600	£1200		
1846		£150	£200	£400	£800
1846	date over inverted 4	Rare			
1846	1 for 1 in date	£600	£1200		
1847		£150	£200	£400	£800
1847	1 for 1 in date	Rare			
1848		£400	£1250	£3000	
1848	2nd larger head	£150	£200	£400	£800
1849		£150	£200	£400	£800
1849	1 for 1 in date	£250	£500	£1000	
1850		£150	£200	£400	£900
1850	1 for 1 in date	£250	£500	£1000	
1851		£130	£175	£300	£600
1852		£130	£160	£275	£500
1852	1 for 1 in date	£250	£500	£1000	
1853		£130	£160	£275	£500
1853	WW incuse	£125	£250	£500	£1000
1854		£130	£175	£300	£600
1854	WW incuse	£120	£160	£300	£650
1855		£150	£300	£600	£1200
1855	WW incuse	£130	£160	£275	£500
1856		£120	£160	£300	£650
1857		£130	£160	£275	£500
1858		£150	£200	£400	£800
1859		£150	£200	£400	£800
1859	Additional line on ribbon	£850	£1750	£3500	
1860		£130	£160	£275	£500
1860	large O	£130	£160	£275	£500
1861		£130	£160	£275	£450
1861	1 for 1 in date	£250	£500	£1000	

Victoria - Young Head, shield reverse
A complicated issue with mint letter, lots of varieties and two entirely different reverses. The first coins listed here are all the shield reverse type, from the London mint.

Date	Notes	F	VF	EF	UNC
1862	Wide date	£130	£160	£250	£400
1862	Narrow date	£130	£160	£250	£400
1863		£130	£160	£250	£400
1863	Roman I for 1	£250	£500	£1000	
1863	'827' on truncation	Rare			

Victoria Young head, shield
back 1852 Sovereign

Die numbers below wreath until 1874

Date	Notes	F	VF	EF	UNC
1863		£130	£160	£250	£400
1863	'827' on truncation, no die No.	Rare			
1864		£130	£160	£225	£400
1865		£130	£175	£300	£600
1866		£130	£160	£225	£400
1866	2nd 6 over 5	£130	£250	£450	£800
1868		£130	£160	£225	£400
1869		£130	£160	£225	£400
1870		£130	£160	£250	£500
1870	WW incuse	£130	£175	£300	£600
1871		£130	£150	£200	£325
1872		£130	£160	£220	£350
1872	No die number (earlier bust)	£130	£220	£300	£550
1873		£130	£160	£220	£350
1874		£1000	£2750	£5000	

Melbourne mint coins, indicated here by an 'M' after the date and distinguished on the coin by a small 'M' under the wreath.

Date	Notes	F	VF	EF	UNC
1872M		£130	£175	£300	£600
1872M	2 over 1	£200	£400	£850	£2000
1874M		£130	£160	£400	£800
1880M		£350	£750	£1750	£3500
1881M		£145	£200	£400	£1200
1882M		£130	£160	£320	£600
1883M		£175	£400	£850	£1750
1884M		£130	£160	£300	£500
1885M		£130	£160	£300	£500
1886M		£700	£2500	£4500	£8000
1887M		£500	£1250	£3250	£6000

The image below shows the die number location on a shield back Victorian sovereign. The number '101' is shown here, but the die numbers do range from very low numbers to 3 digit figures.

They were used in order to log and gain some idea of the speed with which the dies became worn. Interestingly, when the young head Victorian sovereign dies were considered not good enough for use with sovereigns, the obverses were used to strike the obverses of the pre 1860 copper farthings.

Victoria Young head, shield
back 1871 Sovereign

Victoria - Young Head, shield reverse
Sydney mint coins, indicated here by an 'S' after the date and distinguished on the coin by a small 'S' under the wreath.

Date	Notes	F	VF	EF	UNC
1871S		£130	£175	£250	£550
1871S	WW incuse	£130	£175	£300	£650
1872S		£130	£175	£275	£650
1873S		£130	£175	£250	£600
1875S		£130	£175	£250	£500
1877S		£130	£175	£250	£500
1878S		£130	£175	£250	£500
1879S		£130	£175	£250	£500
1880S		£130	£185	£225	£600
1881S		£130	£185	£225	£600
1882S		£130	£185	£225	£550
1883S		£130	£185	£225	£550
1884S		£130	£175	£250	£500
1885S		£130	£175	£250	£500
1886S		£130	£175	£250	£500
1887S		£130	£200	£350	£700

Victoria - Young Head, St George reverse
A change back to the St George reverse now, which is still used today. The shield back coins were produced simultaneously, but were mainly struck in the colonies. London mint coins are listed first.

Date	Notes	F	VF	EF	UNC
1871		BV	£120	£180	£320
1871	Longer horse tail, smaller B.P (approximately the same as above)				
1871	Proof				£5000
1872		BV	£130	£150	£300
1873		BV	£130	£150	£300
1874		BV	£130	£180	£360
1876		BV	£130	£150	£300
1878		BV	£130	£150	£300
1879		£250	£750	£1500	
1880		BV	£130	£150	£300
1880	Short horse tail	BV	£130	£150	£300
1880	no B.P	BV	£130	£185	£360
1880	2nd 8 over 7	£130	£160	£275	£450
1880	2nd 8 over 7, no B.P	£130	£175	£300	£500
1880	Longer horse tail	BV	£130	£150	£300
1884		BV	£130	£150	£300
1885		BV	£130	£150	£300

Victoria - Young Head, St George reverse

Melbourne mint coins, indicated here by an 'M' after the date and distinguished on the coin by a small 'M' under the bust of Queen Victoria.

Date	Notes	F	VF	EF	UNC
1872M		£180	£320	£800	£3000
1873M		BV	£130	£225	£800
1874M		BV	£130	£225	£800
1875M		BV	£130	£200	£700
1876M		BV	£130	£200	£700
1877M		BV	£130	£200	£700
1878M		BV	£130	£175	£600
1879M		BV	£130	£175	£600
1880M		BV	£130	£175	£600
1881M		BV	£130	£175	£600
1881M No B.P		BV	£130	£175	£600
1882M No B.P		BV	£130	£175	£600
1882M		BV	£130	£175	£600
1882M Broader truncation		BV	£130	£175	£600
1883M		BV	£130	£175	£600
1883M Broader truncation		BV	£130	£175	£600
1884M		BV	£130	£175	£600
1884M No B.P		£130	£175	£350	
1884M Broader truncation		BV	£130	£175	£500
1885M		BV	£130	£175	£500
1885M Broader truncation		BV	£130	£175	£500
1886M		BV	£130	£175	£500
1887M		BV	£140	£200	£600

Victoria Young head, St. George
reverse 1879 Melbourne mint Sovereign

The red spot in the image above shows the location of the mint letter when it is present under the bust of Queen Victoria.

Victoria - Young Head, St George reverse

Sydney mint coins, indicated here by an 'S' after the date and distinguished on the coin by a small 'S' under the bust of Queen Victoria.

Date	Notes	F	VF	EF	UNC
1871S	Short horse tail	£130	£185	£500	£1600
1871S	Long horse tail	BV	£160	£400	£1200
1872S		BV	£130	£250	£800
1873S		BV	£130	£300	£900
1874S		BV	£130	£250	£900
1875S		BV	£130	£250	£900
1876S		BV	£130	£250	£750
1879S		£130	£200	£800	£2500
1880S	Long horse tail	BV	£130	£250	£800
1880S	W.W complete	BV	£130	£250	£700
1880S	No B.P	BV	£130	£200	£550
1881S	W.W wide spaced and short (values approximately as above)??				
1881S	W.W complete	BV	£130	£200	£600
1882S	No B.P	BV	£130	£250	£400
1882S		BV	£130	£250	£600
1883S		BV	£130	£300	£1000
1884S		BV	£130	£200	£500
1885S		BV	£130	£200	£500
1886S		BV	£130	£200	£500
1887S		BV	£130	£200	£500

Victoria Young head, St. George
reverse 1887 Sydney mint Sovereign

Victoria - Jubilee Head, St George reverse
London mint coins first.

Date	Notes	F	VF	EF	UNC
1887		BV	£130	£175	£225
1887	Proof				£800
1888		BV	£130	£180	£275
1888	D:G: closer to crown	BV	£130	£180	£275
1889		BV	£130	£175	£250
1890		BV	£130	£175	£250
1891	Short horse tail	£150	£275	£750	
1891	Longer horse tail	BV	£130	£175	£225
1892		BV	£130	£175	£225

Victoria Jubilee head 1893
Sydney mint Sovereign

Melbourne mint coins, indicated here by an 'M' after the date and distinguished on the coin by a small 'M' under the horses rear right hoof.

Date	Notes	F	VF	EF	UNC
1887M		BV	£130	£180	£250
1887M	Small spaced J E B	BV	£150	£200	£275
1888M		BV	£130	£180	£250
1889M		BV	£130	£180	£250
1890M		BV	£130	£180	£250
1891M		BV	£130	£175	£225
1892M		BV	£130	£175	£200
1893M		BV	£130	£175	£250

Sydney mint coins, indicated here by an 'S' after the date and distinguished on the coin by a small 'S' under the horses rear right hoof.

Date	Notes	F	VF	EF	UNC
1887S		BV	£175	£400	£1600
1887S	Proof	Rare			
1888S	Small spaced J E B	BV	£130	£180	£275
1889S		BV	£130	£180	£250
1890S		BV	£130	£180	£250
1891S		BV	£130	£180	£250
1892S		BV	£130	£180	£250
1893S		BV	£130	£180	£250

Victoria - Widow Head, St George reverse
London mint coins first.

Date	Notes	Fine	VF	EF	UNC
1893		BV	BV	£140	£175
1893	Proof				£550
1894		BV	BV	£140	£175
1895		BV	BV	£140	£175
1896		BV	BV	£140	£175
1898		BV	BV	£140	£175
1899		BV	BV	£130	£160
1900		BV	BV	£130	£160
1901		BV	BV	£130	£160

Victoria Veiled head
1900 Sovereign

Melbourne mint coins, indicated here by an 'M' after the date and distinguished
on the coin by a small 'M' under the horses rear right hoof.

Date	Notes	Fine	VF	EF	UNC
1893M		BV	BV	£160	£200
1894M		BV	BV	£140	£175
1895M		BV	BV	£140	£175
1896M		BV	BV	£140	£175
1897M		BV	BV	£140	£175
1898M		BV	BV	£140	£175
1899M		BV	BV	£130	£165
1900M		BV	BV	£130	£165
1901M		BV	BV	£130	£165

Sydney mint coins, indicated here by an 'S' after the date and distinguished
on the coin by a small 'S' under the horses rear right hoof.

Date	Notes	Fine	VF	EF	UNC
1893S		BV	BV	£140	£175
1894S		BV	BV	£140	£175
1895S		BV	BV	£140	£175
1896S		BV	BV	£150	£200
1897S		BV	BV	£160	£180
1898S		BV	BV	£140	£180
1899S		BV	BV	£130	£160
1900S		BV	BV	£130	£160
1901S		BV	BV	£130	£160

Perth mint coins, indicated here by an 'P' after the date and distinguished
on the coin by a small 'P' under the horses rear right hoof.

Date	Notes	Fine	VF	EF	UNC
1899P		£150	£200	£400	£1000
1900P		BV	BV	£140	£200
1901P		BV	BV	£140	£175

dward VII
London mint coins first.

Date	Notes	F	VF	EF	UNC
902	Matte Proof				£250
902		BV	BV	£135	£170
903		BV	BV	£130	£160
904		BV	BV	£130	£160
905		BV	BV	£130	£160
906		BV	BV	£130	£160
907		BV	BV	£130	£160
908		BV	BV	£130	£160
909		BV	BV	£130	£160
910		BV	BV	£130	£160

Edward VII 1902 Sovereign

Ottawa (Canada) mint coins, indicated here by a 'C' after the date and distinguished on the coin by a small 'C' under the horses rear right hoof.

Date	Notes	F	VF	EF	UNC
1908C	Proof				£4000
1909C		BV	£200	£300	£500
1910C		BV	£175	£250	£375

Melbourne mint coins, indicated here by an 'M' after the date and distinguished on the coin by a small 'M' under the horses rear right hoof.

Date	Notes	F	VF	EF	UNC
1902M		BV	BV	£135	£170
1903M		BV	BV	£130	£150
1904M		BV	BV	£130	£150
1905M		BV	BV	£130	£150
1906M		BV	BV	£130	£150
1907M		BV	BV	£130	£150
1908M		BV	BV	£130	£150
1909M		BV	BV	£130	£150
1910M		BV	BV	£130	£150

Above: The enlarged reverse area of a 1902 Sovereign. The red spot shows the location (if present) of the mint letter on St. George reverse sovereigns and half sovereigns from the Jubilee Victoria type to the last colonial mint sovereigns during the reign of George V.

Perth mint coins, indicated here by an 'P' after the date and distinguished on the coin by a small 'P' under the horses rear right hoof.

Date	Notes	F	VF	EF	UNC
1902P		BV	BV	£135	£160
1903P		BV	BV	£130	£150
1904P		BV	BV	£130	£150
1905P		BV	BV	£130	£150
1906P		BV	BV	£130	£150
1907P		BV	BV	£130	£150
1908P		BV	BV	£130	£150
1909P		BV	BV	£130	£150
1910P		BV	BV	£130	£150

Edward VII
Sydney mint coins, indicated here by an 'S' after the date and distinguished on the coin by a small 'S' under the horses rear right hoof.

Date	Notes	F	VF	EF	UNC
1902S		BV	BV	£135	£165
1903S		BV	BV	£135	£165
1904S		BV	BV	£140	£175
1905S		BV	BV	£135	£165
1906S		BV	BV	£135	£165
1907S		BV	BV	£135	£165
1908S		BV	BV	£135	£165
1909S		BV	BV	£135	£165
1910S		BV	BV	£135	£165

George V - London mint coins first

Date	Notes	F	VF	EF	UNC
1911		BV	BV	£125	£135
1911	Proof				£400
1912		BV	BV	£125	£135
1913		BV	BV	£125	£135
1914		BV	BV	£125	£135
1915		BV	BV	£125	£135
1916		BV	BV	£175	£200
1917			£1500	£5000	£10000
1925		BV	BV	£130	£140

George V 1914 Sovereign

Ottawa (Canada) mint coins, indicated here by a 'C' after the date and distinguished on the coin by a small 'C' under the horses rear right hoof.

Date	Notes	F	VF	EF	UNC
1911C		BV	BV	£135	£175
1913C		£350	£700	£1400	
1914C		£200	£400	£800	
1916C		£2000	£4000	£8000	
1917C		BV	£130	£170	£220
1918C		BV	£130	£170	£220
1919C		BV	£130	£175	£230

Bombay (India) mint coins, indicated here by an 'I' after the date and distinguished on the coin by a small 'I' under the horses rear right hoof.

Date	Notes	F	VF	EF	UNC
1918I		BV	BV	£130	£150

Melbourne mint coins, indicated here by an 'M' after the date and distinguished on the coin by a small 'M' under the horses rear right hoof.

Date	Notes	F	VF	EF	UNC
1911M		BV	BV	£125	£135
1912M		BV	BV	£125	£135
1913M		BV	BV	£125	£135
1914M		BV	BV	£125	£140
1915M		BV	BV	£125	£140

George V

Date	Notes	F	VF	EF	UNC
1916M		BV	BV	£130	£150
1917M		BV	BV	£130	£150
1918M		BV	BV	£130	£150
1919M		BV	£130	£200	£275
1920M		£750	£1500	£3000	
1921M		Rare			
1922M		Rare			
1923M		BV	£130	£160	£185
1924M		BV	£140	£180	£225
1925M		BV	BV	£130	£165
1926M		BV	£140	£180	£225
1928M		Rare			
1929M		£600	£1000		
1930M		BV	£140	£200	£250
1931M		£160	£225	£325	£450

Perth mint coins, indicated here by a 'P' after the date and distinguished on the coin by a small 'P' under the horses rear right hoof.

Date	Notes	F	VF	EF	UNC
1911P		BV	BV	£125	£135
1912P		BV	BV	£125	£135
1913P		BV	BV	£125	£135
1914P		BV	BV	£125	£135
1915P		BV	BV	£125	£135
1916P		BV	BV	£130	£145
1917P		BV	BV	£130	£145
1918P		BV	BV	£125	£135
1919P		BV	BV	£135	£145
1920P		BV	BV	£135	£145
1921P		BV	BV	£135	£160
1922P		BV	BV	£130	£145
1923P		BV	BV	£130	£145
1924P		£130	£160	£180	£225
1925P		£200	£400	£1000	£1500
1926P		£200	£400	£1000	£1500
1927P		£130	£180	£320	£450
1928P		BV	£140	£200	£275
1929P		BV	BV	£150	£200
1930P		BV	BV	£150	£180
1931P		BV	BV	£150	£180

Sydney mint coins, indicated here by an 'S' after the date and distinguished on the coin by a small 'S' under the horses rear right hoof.

Date	Notes	F	VF	EF	UNC
1911S		BV	BV	£125	£135
1912S		BV	BV	£125	£135
1913S		BV	BV	£125	£135
1914S		BV	BV	£130	£140
1915S		BV	BV	£125	£135
1916S		BV	BV	£135	£150

George V

Date	Notes	F	VF	EF	UNC
1917S		BV	BV	£135	£150
1918S		BV	BV	£130	£140
1919S		BV	BV	£135	£160
1920S		Rare			
1921S		£450	£800	£1200	£1800
1922S		£3000	£5000		
1923S		£3000	£5000		
1924S		£400	£600	£850	£1350
1925S		BV	BV	£140	£180
1926S		£5000	£10000		

Pretoria (South Africa) mint coins, indicated by an 'SA' after the date and distinguished by a small 'SA' under the horses rear right hoof.

Date	Notes	F	VF	EF	UNC
1923SA		£1000	£2000		
1923SA	Proof				£750
1924SA		£1500	£3500		
1925SA		BV	BV	£130	£140
1926SA		BV	BV	£130	£140
1927SA		BV	BV	£130	£140
1928SA		BV	BV	£130	£140
1929SA		BV	BV	£130	£140
1930SA		BV	BV	£130	£140
1931SA		BV	BV	£130	£140
1932SA		BV	BV	£140	£165

George V 1931 Pretoria mint (SA) Sovereign

Edward VIII
Extremely rare, not to be confused with modern fantasy patterns.

George VI
This issue was a plain edged proof only, struck in London. 5001 were struck, the odd '1' was for the King himself.

Date	Notes	F	VF	EF	UNC
1937	Plain edge Proof				£1500

George VI 1937 Proof and Elizabeth II first bust Sovereign obverses.

Elizabeth II

Date	Notes	F	VF	EF	UNC
1957		BV	BV	BV	£130
1958		BV	BV	BV	£130
1959		BV	BV	£110	£130
1962		BV	BV	BV	£130
1963		BV	BV	BV	£125
1964		BV	BV	BV	£125
1965		BV	BV	BV	£125
1966		BV	BV	BV	£125
1967		BV	BV	BV	£125
1968		BV	BV	BV	£125
(Decimal 1974 to 1982*)		BV	BV	BV	£125

*Coins were not struck every year.

George III

Date	Notes	F	VF	EF	UNC
1820	Pattern/Proof only	Rare			

George IV

Date	Notes	F	VF	EF	UNC
1823	St. George reverse	£750	£1500	£3000	
1826	Proof (illustrated)				£4000
Other dates/proofs all very rare					

George IV 1825 Proof Two Pound Coin

William IV

Date	Notes	F	VF	EF	UNC
1831	Proof				£4000

Victoria

Date	Notes	F	VF	EF	UNC
1887	Jubilee Head	£280	£360	£400	£550
1887	Jubilee Head Proof				£1000
1893	Veiled Head	£280	£400	£650	£1000
1893	Veiled Head Proof				£1500

Edward VII

Date	Notes	F	VF	EF	UNC
1902		£250	£300	£450	£650
1902	Proof				£550

George V

Date	Notes	F	VF	EF	UNC
1911	Proof				£800

Edward VII
Not issued.

George VI

Date	Notes	F	VF	EF	UNC
1937	Proof				£600

Elizabeth II
None until 1980.

orge VI 1937 Proof Two Pound Coin

George III

Date	Notes	F	VF	EF	UNC
1820	Pattern/Proof only	Rare			

George IV

Date	Notes	F	VF	EF	UNC
1826	Patten/Proof only				£10000

William IV
Not issued.

Victoria

Date	Notes	F	VF	EF	UNC
1839	Young head, proof only				£25000+
1887	Jubilee Head	£600	£750	£900	£1250
1887	Jubilee Head Proof				£2800
1893	Veiled Head	£600	£1000	£1500	£2500
1893	Veiled Head Proof				£3750

Edward VII

Date	Notes	F	VF	EF	UNC
1902		£600	£700	£900	£1200
1902	Proof				£1000

George V

Date	Notes	F	VF	EF	UNC
1911	Proof				£2000

Edward VIII
Not issued.

George VI

Date	Notes	F	VF	EF	UNC
1937	Proof				£1000

Elizabeth II
None until 1980.

Victoria 1887 Five Pound Coin

George V 1911 Proof
Five Pound Coin obverse

Proof Section: Rare Proofs and some Pattern Coins

This section is organised in much the same way as the previous with the exception that the monarchs are no longer split up, and grade columns are not included because more often than not proof coins are collected/found in higher grades. Many of these coins are very rare and it is important to bear in mind that the prices may not be accurate with coins that are rarely seen for sale. Peck numbers are stated for all copper coins, ESC numbers for silver coins, and both Peck and Freeman for bronze coins. The coins are the same in appearance as the normal currency issues unless otherwise stated. The emphasis in this section is on Proof coins rather than patterns. Please also be aware that it is beyond the scope of this book to list all known proofs, especially those that are rarely seen, and readers are referred to the more advanced reference books listed in the bibliography.

Date	Type	Peck	Estimated Rarity	Value (AFDC)
Quarter Farthings				
1852	Bronzed Proof	P1611	Extremely Rare	
1853	Bronzed Proof	P1613	Extremely Rare	
Third Farthings				
1827	Copper Proof	P1454	Extremely Rare	
1835	Copper Proof	P1478	Rare	
1866	Bronze Proof	P1927	Extremely Rare	
1868	Bronze Proof	P1929	Very Rare	
1868	Cu-Ni Proof	P1930	Very Rare	£200+
1868	Aluminium Proof	P1931	Excessively Rare	£450+
1881	Bronze Proof	P1935	Extremely Rare	
Half Farthings				
1828	Bronzed Proof	P1447	Extremely Rare	£500+
1828	Copper Proof	P1448	Very Rare	£250+
1830	Copper Proof	P1452	Very Rare	£250+
1839	Bronzed Proof	P1591	Extremely Rare	£250+
1853	Bronzed Proof	P1600	Extremely Rare	£300+
1853	Copper Proof	P1601	Very Rare	£250+
1868	Cu-Ni Proof	P1604	Very Rare	£500+
1868	Bronze Proof	P1605	Very Rare	£500+
Farthings				
1797	Many Pattern 'Cartwheel' Farthings in various metals.			All £300+
Noted:				
1797	Copper Proof	P1199A	Very Rare	£450 (AFDC)
1797	Silver Proof	P1197	Excessively Rare	£1850 (AFDC)
1797	Gilt Copper Proof	P1188	Extremely Rare	£650 (AFDC)
1798	Many Pattern 'Cartwheel' Farthings in various metals.			All £300+
Noted:				
1798	Gilt Copper Proof	P1202	Extremely Rare	£425
1798	Silver Proof	P1206A	Exceedingly Rare	£2000 ??
1799	Copper, Gilt and Bronzed Proofs exist			£200+ FDC

Coins not intended for circulation - Farthings (continued)

Date	Type	Peck	Estimated Rarity	Value (AFDC+)
1799	Bronzed Proof	P1273	Very Rare	£175 (NFDC)
1799	Copper Proof	P1274	Very Rare	£175 (GEF)
1799	Bronzed Proof	P1277	Very Rare	£150 (NFDC)
1805	Pattern Bronzed restrike		Very Rare	£350+
1805	Silver Restrike	P1318	Extremely Rare	£2000 ??
1806	Copper, Gilt, Bronzed, Silver and even Gold Proofs exist.			£200-£2000 approx
Noted:				
1806	Bronzed Copper Proof	P1387	Very Rare	£225
1806	Bronzed Copper Proof	P1388	Very Rare	£150 (NFDC)
1806	Copper Proof	P1389	Rare	£150 (AFDC)
1806	Bronzed Copper Proof	P1406	Very Rare	£250 (AFDC)
1807	Restrikes in various metals exist			£300-£1000 approx
None	Trial Coin, blank Rev	P1417	Excessively Rare	£2000 ??
1821	Copper Proof	P1408	Very Rare	£450+
1821	Bronzed copper Proof	P1418	Excessively Rare	£1000+ ??
1822	Copper Proof	P1410	Extremely Rare	£450+
1825	Gold Proof	P1415	Excessively Rare	£4000 ??
1826	Bronzed copper Proof	P1440	Rare	£200+
1826	Copper Proof	P1441	Very Rare	£200+
1831	Bronzed copper Proof	P1457	Very Rare	£250+
1831	Bronzed copper Proof	P1458	Rare (up/down align)	£200+
1831	Copper Proof	P1459	Extremely Rare	£400+
1839	Silver Proof	P1555	Excessively Rare	£2000 ??
1839	Bronzed copper Proof	P1556	Rare	£220
1839	Bronzed Proof	P1557	Very Rare (up/down align)	£250 ?
1839	Copper Proof	P1558	Extremely Rare	£1000+ ??
1841	Copper Proof	P1561	Extremely Rare	£1000+
1853	Bronzed copper Proof	P1576	Very Rare	£250+ ??
1853	Copper Proof	P1577	Extremely Rare	£500+ (raised WW)
1853	Copper Proof	P1579	Rare	£450 (incuse WW)
1860	Copper Proof (Young Head)	ND	Excessively Rare	£6000 ??

Date	Type	Peck/FMAN	Rarity	Value
1860	Bronze Proof	P1856/497A?	Excessively Rare	£350 (Bun head)
1860	Bronzed copper Proof	P1857/500?	Excessively Rare	£300+ ?? (Bun)
1861	Gold Proof	P1862/504	Excessively Rare	£2000+ ??
1861	Silver Proof	P1863/505	Excessively Rare	£2000+ ??
1861	Bronze Proof	P1864/506	Extremely Rare	£350
1862	Bronze Proof	P1866/508	Extremely Rare	£300+
1863	Bronze Proof	P1868/510	Extremely Rare	£300+
1866	Bronze Proof	P1877/515	Extremely Rare	£300+
1867	Bronzed copper Proof	P1879/517	Extremely Rare	£350+
1867	Bronze Proof	P1880/518	Extremely Rare	£350+
1868	Bronze Proof	P1882/521?	Extremely Rare	£300+
Freeman lists an 1868 Copper Proof, is this the Peck Bronze Proof??				
1868	Cu-Ni Proof	P1883/520	Excessively Rare	£500+
1874H	Bronze Proof	P1889/526	Excessively Rare	£250+
1875H	Bronze Proof	P1893/533	Excessively Rare	£250+ ??
1877	Bronze Proof	P1895/535	Excessively Rare	£2500+
1878	Bronze Proof	P1897/537	Excessively Rare	£350+

Coins not intended for circulation - Farthings (continued)

Date	Type	Peck/FMAN	Estimated Rarity	Value (AFDC - FDC)
1879	Bronze Proof	ND/539	Excessively Rare	£300+ ??
1879	Bronze Proof	ND/540A	Excessively Rare	£300+(large 9)
1880	Bronze Proof	P1900/543A	Excessively Rare	£300+ ??
1881	Bronze Proof	P1903/547	Excessively Rare	£300+ ??
1882H	Bronze Proof	P1906/550	Excessively Rare	£300+ ??
1883	Bronze Proof	P1908/552	Excessively Rare	£300+ ??
1884	Bronze Proof	P1910/554	Excessively Rare	£300+ ?
1885	Bronze Proof	P1912/556	Excessively Rare	£300+ ??
1886	Bronze Proof	P1914/558	Excessively Rare	£300+ ??
1890	Bronze Proof	P1918/563	Excessively Rare	£300+ ??
1891	Bronze Proof	P1920/565	Excessively Rare	£300+ ??
1892	Bronze Proof	P1922/567	Excessively Rare	£300+ ??
1895	Very Prooflike	ND/ND	Scarce	£40
(Above is probably an early striking using non proof dies).				
1896	Bronze Proof	P1960/573	Very Rare	£250+ ??
1901	Bronze Proof	P1967/ND	Extremely Rare	£250+ ??
1902	Undarkened Proof	P2232/ND	Excessively Rare	£300+ ??
1926	Bronze Proof	P2339/606	Extremely Rare	£200-300
1927	Bronze Proof	P2341/608	Extremely Rare	£200-300
1928	Bronze Proof	P2343/610	Extremely Rare	£200-300
1929	Bronze Proof	P2345/612	Extremely Rare	£200-300
1930	Bronze Proof	P2347/614	Extremely Rare	£200-300
1931	Bronze Proof	P2349/616	Extremely Rare	£200-300
1932	Bronze Proof	P2351/618	Extremely Rare	£200-300
1933	Bronze Proof	P2353/620	Extremely Rare	£200-300
1934	Bronze Proof	P2355/622	Extremely Rare	£200-300
1935	Bronze Proof	P2357/624	Extremely Rare	£200-300
1936	Bronze Proof	P2364/626	Extremely Rare	£200-300
1937	Bronze Proof	Proof from set, see Main section.		
1938	Bronze Proof	P2460/631	Extremely Rare	Approx £300
1939	Bronze Proof	P2462/633	Extremely Rare	Approx £300
1940	Bronze Proof	P2464/635	Extremely Rare	Approx £300
1941	Bronze Proof	P2466/637	Extremely Rare	Approx £300
1942	Bronze Proof	P2468/639	Extremely Rare	Approx £300
1943	Bronze Proof	P2470/641	Extremely Rare	Approx £300
1944	Bronze Proof	P2472/643	Extremely Rare	Approx £300
1945	Bronze Proof	P2474/645	Extremely Rare	Approx £300
1946	Bronze Proof	P2476/647	Extremely Rare	Approx £300
1947	Bronze Proof	P2478/649	Extremely Rare	Approx £300
1948	Bronze Proof	P2480/651	Extremely Rare	Approx £300
1949	Bronze Proof	P2482/653	Extremely Rare	Approx £300
1950	Bronze Proof	P2484/655	Extremely Rare	Approx £300
1951	Bronze Proof	P2486/657	Extremely Rare	Approx £300
1952	Bronze Proof	P2488/659	Extremely Rare	Approx £300
1953	Bronze Proof	Proof from set, see Main section.		
1954	Bronze Proof	P2524/666	Extremely Rare	£300 ??
1955	Bronze Proof	P2526/668	Extremely Rare	£300 ??
1956	Bronze Proof	P2528/670	Extremely Rare	£300 ??

Coins not intended for circulation - Halfpennies

Date	Type	Peck	Estimated Rarity	Value (AFDC+)
1797+	Many 'Cartwheelesque' patterns exist in various metals for 1797 and 1798, and 1798+ proofs/patterns similar to the circulation type exist in many different metals for 1799+1799 All are at least very rare, and Peck should be consulted to aid identification of these coins. Speculation and recent prices would lead me to believe that each would probably be worth at least £300, with rarer types being worth considerably more. Notable examples include:			
1797	Copper Pattern	P1154	Very Rare	Approx £250+ (VF)
1799	Gilt Pattern	P1156	Very Rare	Approx £500+
1799	Gilt Pattern	P1233	Very Rare	Approx £120+ (EF)
1799	Bronzed Copper Pattern	P1234	Very Rare	Approx £250+
1799	Copper pattern	P1235	Very Rare	Approx £250+
1799	Bronzed Copper Pattern	P1247	Very Rare	Approx £250+
1805	Various patterns and proofs exist in various metals, all are at least very rare and would probably sell for £250 - £500. Restrikes also exist. Peck should be consulted.			
1806	As 1805, proofs and restrike proofs in various metals exist. Values are probably in the region of £300-£500 for many types.			
1807	Restrike Gold Proof	P1381	Excessively Rare	
1807	Restrike Silver Proof	P1382	Excessively Rare	
1807	Restrike Bronzed Proof	P1383	Very Rare	
1807	Restrike Copper Proof	P1384	Very Rare	
1807	Restrike Aluminium Proof	P1385	Extremely Rare	
1825	Copper Proof	P1421	Very Rare	
1826	Bronzed Copper Proof	P1423/P1426/P1428*	Very Rare	£300+ (FDC)
	* For 1826 Proofs, varieties with the saltire exist just as with the currency coins.			
1826	Copper Proof	P1424	Very Rare	
1826	Copper Proof	P1429	Extremely Rare	£600+ ??
	With thick line down arms of saltire.			
1831	Bronzed Copper Proof	P1462	Very Rare	£300+
	With Up/Up alignment (see appendix 1)			
1831	Bronzed Copper Proof	P1463	Rare	£400+
	With Up/Down alingnment (see appendix 1)			
1839	Bronzed Copper Proof	P1523	Very Rare	£300+
	With Up/Up alingnment (see appendix 1)			
1839	Bronzed Copper Proof	P1524	Very Rare	£300+
	With Up/Down alignment			
1841	Silver Proof	P1525	Excessively Rare	£2000+
1841	Bronzed Copper Proof	P1526	Very Rare	£300+??
1853	Bronzed Copper Proof	P1540	Very Rare	£400+
1853	Copper Proof	P1541	Very Rare	£250+

Date	Type	Peck/FMAN	Rarity	Value (AFDC-FDC)
1860	Bronze proofs and copper proofs with a bronzed finish exist for 3 of the subtle obverse/reverse combinations. All are extremely rare. £500-£700 approx.			
1861	Bronze Proof	P1768/271	Excessively Rare	
1861	Bronze Proof	P1772/287	Excessively Rare	
	Freeman Obv 7 with all leaf veins in relief.			

Coins not intended for circulation - Halfpennies (Continued)

Date	Type	Peck/FMAN	Rarity	Value (AFDC-FDC)
1861	Gold, Silver, Cupro-Nickel and Brass proofs exist. All are excessively rare.			
			Approx	£500-£1000+
1862	Bronze Proof	P1775/290*	Extremely Rare	£300+
1862	Bronze Proof	P1777/291*	Extremely Rare	£300+
* Latter has Freeman reverse H				
1863	Bronze Proof	P1780/294A	Extremely Rare	£300+
1864	Bronze Proof	ND/295A	Excessively Rare	£500+ ??
1866	Bronze Proof	P1786/299	Extremely Rare	£300+ ??
1867	Bronzed Copper Proof	P1789/301	Extremely Rare	
1867	Bronze Proof	P1790/302	Excessively Rare	
1868	Bronze Proof	P1793/305	Extremely Rare	£350 ??
1868	Cu-Ni Proof	P1794/304	Extremely Rare	£350+
1872	Brass Proof	P1799/309A	Excessively Rare	£1000+ ??
1874H	Bronze Proof	P1807/319	Extremely Rare	£300+
1875H	Bronze Proof	P1812/324	Excessively Rare	£500+ ??
1876	Bronze Proof	ND/329A	Excessively Rare	
1877	Bronze Proof	P1818/331	Extremely Rare	
1878	Bronze Proof	P1822/336	Extremely Rare	
1880	Bronze Proof	P1828/341	Extremely Rare	
1881	Bronze Proof	P1830/343*	Extremely Rare	
1881	Bronze Proof	ND/345*	Excessively Rare	
* Freeman 345 has a brooch at the neckline of the Queen, not a rose as on 343.				
1882H	Bronze Proof	P1832/346	Extremely Rare	
1883	Bronze Proof	P1834/350	Extremely Rare	
1884	Bronze Proof	P1838/353	Extremely Rare	
1885	Bronze Proof	P1840/355	Extremely Rare	
1886	Bronze Proof	P1842/357	Extremely Rare	
1887	Bronze Proof	ND/358A	Extremely Rare	
1889	Bronze Proof 9/8	ND/361A	Excessively Rare	
1890	Bronze Proof	P1847/363	Extremely Rare	
1891	Bronze Proof	P1849/365	Extremely Rare	
1892	Bronze Proof	P1851/367	Extremely Rare	
1893	Bronze Proof	ND/368A	Extremely Rare	
1894	Bronze Proof	ND/369A	Extremely Rare	
1895	Bronze Proof	ND/370A	Extremely Rare	
1896	Bronze Proof	ND/371A	Extremely Rare	
1900	Bronze Proof	ND/377A	Extremely Rare	
1901	Bronze Proof	P1957/379	Extremely Rare	
1902	Bronze Proof	P2222/ND	Extremely Rare	
1926	Bronze Proof	P2303/407	Extremely Rare	£300 ??
1927	Bronze Proof	P2305/409	Extremely Rare	£300 ??
1928	Bronze Proof	P2307/411	Extremely Rare	£300 ??
1929	Bronze Proof	P2309/413	Extremely Rare	£300 ??
1930	Bronze Proof	P2311/415	Extremely Rare	£300 ??
1931	Bronze Proof	P2313/417	Extremely Rare	£300 ??
1932	Bronze Proof	P2315/419	Extremely Rare	£300 ??
1933	Bronze Proof	P2317/421	Extremely Rare	£300 ??
1934	Bronze Proof	P2319/423	Extremely Rare	£300 ??
1935	Bronze Proof	P2321/425	Extremely Rare	£300 ??
1936	Bronze Proof GV	P2362/427	Extremely Rare	£300 ??
1937	Proof from set, see main section.			

Coins not intended for circulation - Halfpennies (Continued)

Date	Type	Peck/FMAN	Rarity	Value (AFDC-FDC)
1938	Bronze Proof	P2427/432	Extremely Rare	£300 ??
1939	Bronze Proof	P2429/434	Extremely Rare	£300 ??
1940	Bronze Proof	P2431/436	Extremely Rare	£300 ??
1941	Bronze Proof	P2433/440	Extremely Rare	£300 ??
1942	Bronze Proof	P2435/442	Extremely Rare	£300 ??
1943	Bronze Proof	P2437/444	Extremely Rare	£300 ??
1944	Bronze Proof	P2439/446	Extremely Rare	£300 ??
1945	Bronze Proof	P2441/448	Extremely Rare	£300 ??
1946	Bronze Proof	P2443/450	Extremely Rare	£300 ??
1947	Bronze Proof	P2445/452	Extremely Rare	£300 ??
1948	Bronze Proof	P2447/454	Extremely Rare	£300 ??
1949	Bronze Proof	P2449/456	Extremely Rare	£300 ??
1950	Proof from set, see main section.			
1951	Proof from set, see main section.			
1952	Bronze Proof	P2455/462	Extremely Rare	£300 ??
1953	Proof from set, see main section.			
1953	Bronze Proof	ND/465A*	Very Rare	£170
	* Smaller design than the proof from set, the base of the sea to the top of the ship measures 18.8mm, whereas, it is 19.25mm on the 1953 proof from the set.			
1954	Bronze Proof	P2509/467	Extremely Rare	£200 ??
1955	Bronze Proof	P2512/470	Extremely Rare	£200 ??
1956	Bronze Proof	P2514/472	Extremely Rare	£200 ??
1957	Bronze Proof	P2517/478	Extremely Rare	£200 ??
1958	Bronze Proof	P2519/482	Extremely Rare	£200 ??
1959	Bronze Proof	P2519B/484	Extremely Rare	£200 ??
1960	Bronze Proof	P2519D/486	Extremely Rare	£200 ??
1962	Bronze Proof	P2519F/488	Extremely Rare	£200 ??
1963	Bronze Proof	P2519H/490	Extremely Rare	£200 ??
1964	Bronze Proof	ND/491A	Extremely Rare	£200 ??
1965	Gold Proof	ND	Excessively Rare	£1500+ ??
1966	Nickel-Brass Proof	ND	Excessively Rare	£400+
1966	Aluminium Proof	ND	Excessively Rare	£350+

Pennies

Date	Type	Peck	Rarity	Value (AFDC-FDC)
1797	Many proofs and restrikes in various metals including silver, gold, gilt copper, bronzed copper and tin. It is beyond the scope of this book to list all types, and readers are referred to the C Wilson Peck book. See bibliography.			
Noted are:				
1797	Gold Proof	P1111 ?	Excessively Rare	£20,000 approx
1797	Bronzed Copper Proof	ND	Extremely Rare	£300+
1797	Bronze Proof	P1118	Extremely Rare	£450 AFDC (2005)
1805	As with 1797, many patterns exist in various metals.			
1806	Many Proofs of various metals exist, noted are:			
1806	Gilt Copper Proof	P1325	Very Rare	£400+
1806	Copper Proof	P1327	Very Rare	£400+ UNC (EF £150)
1806	Bronzed Copper Proof	P1333	Very Rare	£150+ (EF)
1807	Gilt Copper Proof	P1344	Excessively Rare	
1807	Bronzed Copper Proof	P1345	Extremely Rare	

Coins not intended for circulation - Pennies (Continued)

Date	Type	Peck	Rarity	Value (AFDC-FDC)
1807	Restrike in various metals also exist.			
1825	Copper Proof	P1421	Very Rare	£300+
1826	Bronzed Copper Proof	P1423 (Rev A)	Very Rare	
1826	Bronzed Copper Proof	P1426 (Rev B)	Very Rare	
1826	Bronzed Copper Proof	P1428 (Rev C)	Very Rare	
1826	Copper Proof	P1424 (Rev A)	Very Rare	
1826	Copper Proof	P1429 (Rev C)	Very Rare	

Reverse types for 1826: A = No central line down arms of saltire. B = Thin raised line down arms of saltire.
C = Thick raised line down arms of saltire. The saltire is the cross of St. Andrew as part of the Union flag on
Britannia's shield.

Date	Type	Peck	Rarity	Value (AFDC-FDC)
1831	Bronzed Copper Proof	P1462*	Very Rare	£300+
	Up/Up alignment. See appendix I.			
1831	Bronzed Copper Proof	P1463*	Very Rare	£300+
	Up/Down alignment. See appendix I.			
1839	Bronzed Copper Proof	P1479	Very Rare	£450+
1841	Silver Proof	P1481	Excessively Rare	£2000 ??
1841	Bronzed Copper Proof	P1482	Very Rare	£400+
1841	Copper Proof	P1483	Extremely Rare	£400+
1844	Copper Proof	P1488	Unconfirmed	
1853	Bronzed Copper Proof	P1501	Extremely Rare	£500 FDC
1853	Copper Proof	P1502	Very Rare	£500
1856	Copper Proof	P1511	Excessively Rare	£500+
1859	Copper Proof	P1520	Excessively Rare	Approx £750+

Bronze type from here.
For more information on the different types of 1860 and 1861 proofs, refer to the Bronze Coinage of Great Britain
by Michael J Freeman.

Date	Type	Peck	Rarity	Value (AFDC-FDC)
1860	Gold Proof	P1620A/2	Excessively Rare	£15,000+ ??
1860	Silver Proof	P1621/3	Excessively Rare	£750+
1860	Bronzed Copper Proof	P1622/4	Extremely Rare	£1200
1860	Bronzed Copper Proof	ND/5 thick flan. Extremely Rare		
1860	Bronze Proof	ND/6A	Extremely Rare	
1860	Bronzed Bronze Proof	ND/8C	Extremely Rare	
1860	Bronze Proof	P1631/12	Very Rare	£250+
1861	Bronze Proof	P1645/31	Extremely Rare	
1861	Gold Proof	P1647/34	Excessively Rare	
1861	Silver Proof	P1648/35	Excessively Rare	
1861	Silver Proof	P1650/35A		
	Last 1 of date low and double cut		Excessively Rare	
1861	Bronzed Copper Proof	P1651/36		
	Last 1 of date low and double cut		Extremely Rare	
1861	Copper Proof	P1652?/37A?		
	Last 1 of date low and double cut Extremely Rare			

Peck lists a bronze proof but no copper proof, so could the bronze proof be copper or vice versa? Is either Peck
or Freeman incorrect?

Date	Type	Peck	Rarity	Value (AFDC-FDC)
1862	Bronze Proof	P1654/39A	Extremely Rare	£400+
1863	Bronze Proof	P1660/43	Extremely Rare	£300+
1867	Bronzed Copper Proof	P1680/54	Extremely Rare	
1867	Bronze Proof	P1681/55	Extremely Rare	
1867	Silver Proof	ND/ND ??	Unique?	£700+
1868	Bronze Proof	P1683/58	Extremely Rare	£750
1868	Cu-Ni Proof	P1684/57	Extremely Rare	£400+

Coins not intended for circulation - Pennies (Continued)

Date	Type	Peck/FMAN	Rarity	Value (AFDC-FDC)
1868	Copper Proof	ND/58A	Extremely Rare	
1872	Bronze Proof	ND/63	Excessively Rare	
1874H	Bronze Proof	P1698/74	Extremely Rare	£720
1875	Bronze Proof	P1702/81	Excessively Rare	
1875	Cu-Ni Proof	P1704/83	Excessively Rare	
1875	Bronze thicker Proof	ND/84	Excessively Rare	
1875H	Bronze Proof	P1706/86	Extremely Rare	£600
1876H	Bronze Proof*	ND/88 Rev J	Excessively Rare	
1876H	Bronze Proof*	ND/89A Rev K	Excessively Rare	

*Subtle reverse differences, please refer to Freeman.

Date	Type	Peck/FMAN	Rarity	Value (AFDC-FDC)
1877	Bronze Proof	P1710/92	Excessively Rare	
1877	Cu-Ni Proof	P1711/91	Excessively Rare	£700 (NFDC)
1878	Bronze Proof	P1713/95	Excessively Rare	£300
1879	Bronze Proof	ND/97A	Excessively Rare	
1880	Bronze Proof	P1718/100	Excessively Rare	£500
1880	Bronze Proof*	ND/101A	Excessively Rare	£700 ??

* Subtle reverse differences, please refer to Freeman.

Date	Type	Peck/FMAN	Rarity	Value (AFDC-FDC)
1881	Bronze Proof	P1721/104	Excessively Rare	£2400
1881	Bronze Proof	P1723/107	Excessively Rare	£1350
1881	Bronze Proof	P1725/110	Possibly only 2	£3600
1882H	Bronze Proof	P1727/113	Excessively Rare	£1000 ??
1883	Bronze Proof	P1731/117	Excessively Rare	£1000 ??
1884	Bronze Proof	P1734/120	Excessively Rare	£1000 ??
1885	Bronze Proof	P1736/122	Excessively Rare	£1000 ??
1886	Bronze Proof	P1738/124	Excessively Rare	£1000 ??
1889	Bronze Proof*	P1741B/129	Excessively Rare	£1000 ??
1889	Bronze Proof*	ND/127A	Excessively Rare	£1000 ??

* Freeman 129 has 14 leaves in the wreath, 127A has 15.

Date	Type	Peck/FMAN	Rarity	Value (AFDC-FDC)
1890	Bronze Proof	P1743/131	Excessively Rare	£500 ??
1891	Bronze Proof	P1745/133	Excessively Rare	£500 ??
1892	Bronze Proof	P1747/135	Excessively Rare	£500 ??
1893	Bronze Proof	ND/137	Excessively Rare	
1894	Bronze Proof	ND/138A	Excessively Rare	
1895	Bronze Proof*	P1940/140	Excessively Rare	
1895	Bronze Proof*	P1941*/142	Excessively Rare	

* P1941*/142 is low tide type.

Date	Type	Peck/FMAN	Rarity	Value (AFDC-FDC)
1896	Bronze Proof	ND/143A	Excessively Rare	
1900	Bronze Proof	ND/153A	Excessively Rare	
1901	Bronze Proof	P1949/155	Excessively Rare	£300+
1902	Bronze Proof	P2207/ND	Excessively Rare	
1908	Bronze Proof	P2217/167	Excessively Rare	£700+ ??
1926	Bronze Proof	P2264/194	Excessively Rare	£300+
1926	Bronze Proof*	P2266/196	Excessively Rare	£300+

* Modified Effigy.

Date	Type	Peck/FMAN	Rarity	Value (AFDC-FDC)
1927	Bronze Proof	P2268/198	Excessively Rare	£300+
1928	Bronze Proof	P2270/200	Excessively Rare	£300+
1929	Bronze Proof	P2272/202	Excessively Rare	£300+
1930	Bronze Proof	P2274/204	Excessively Rare	£300+
1931	Bronze Proof	P2276/206	Excessively Rare	£300+
1932	Bronze Proof	P2278/208	Excessively Rare	£300+
1934	Bronze Proof*	P2281/211	Excessively Rare	£300+

* Peck lists the 1934 Proof as a Bronzed Proof.

Coins not intended for circulation - Pennies (Continued)

Date	Type	Peck/FMAN	Rarity	Value (AFDC-FDC)
1935	Bronze Proof	P2283/213	Excessively Rare	£300+
1936	Bronze Proof	P2360/215	Excessively Rare	£300+
1937	Bronze Proof (EDVIII)	P2367/216	Excessively Rare	£20,000+
1937	George VI, Proof from set, see Main section.			
1938	Bronze Proof	P2403/223	Excessively Rare	£300+ ??
1939	Bronze Proof	P2405/225	Excessively Rare	£300+ ??
1940	Bronze Proof	P2408/228	Excessively Rare	£300+ ??
1944	Bronze Proof	P2410/230	Excessively Rare	£300+ ??
1945	Bronze Proof	P2412/232	Excessively Rare	£300+ ??
1946	Bronze Proof	P2414/234	Excessively Rare	£300+ ??
1947	Bronze Proof	ND/235A	Excessively Rare	£300+ ??
1948	Bronze Proof	P2417/237	Excessively Rare	£300+ ??
1949	Bronze Proof	P2419/239	Excessively Rare	£300+ ??
1950	Proof from set, see main section.			
1951	Proof from set, see main section.			
1953	Proof from set, see main section.			
1961	Bronze Proof	P2504B/249	Excessively Rare	
1962	Bronze Proof	P2504D/251	Excessively Rare	
1963	Bronze Proof	P2504F/253	Excessively Rare	
1964	Bronze Proof	ND/254A	Excessively Rare	
1965	Gold Proof	ND	Unique?	£2500+
1970	Proof from set, see main section.			

Threehalfpences

Date	Type	ESC	Rarity	Value (AFDC-FDC)
1843	Silver Proof	2259A	Excessively Rare	£500 ??
1843	Silver Proof 43/34	2259C	Excessively Rare	£500+
1862	Silver Proof	2261A	Excessively Rare	£500+
1870	Silver Proof	2262	Excessively Rare	£1000

Twopences (Cartwheel)

Date	Type	Peck	Rarity	Value (AFDC-FDC)
1797	Proofs and restrikes of many different metals including gold, silver, gilt and bronzed copper exist. The reader is referred to Peck for more details. Noted are:			
1797	Bronzed Copper Proof	P1065	Extremely Rare	£800+
1797	Bronzed Copper Proof	P1068	Extremely Rare	£600
1797	Bronzed Copper Proof	P1075	Extremely Rare	£500

Coins not intended for circulation - Threepences (Silver type)

Date	Type	ESC	Rarity	Value (AFDC-FDC)
1879	Silver Proof	2086	Extremely Rare	
1885	Silver Proof	2092A	Excessively Rare	
1887	Silver Proof (Young head)	2095	Extremely Rare	
1887	Jubilee Head Proof from set, see main section.			
1893	Old Head Proof from set, see main section.			
1902	Edward VII Proof from set, see main section.			
1911	George V Proof from set, see main section.			
1923	Nickel proof	2149A	Excessively Rare	
1925	Nickel Proof	2149B	Excessively Rare	
1925	Matt Nickel Proof	2149C	Excessively Rare	
1927	George V Proof from set, see Main section.			
1927	Matt Silver Proof	2141A	Excessively Rare	
1934	Silver Proof	ND	Unique?	£300+
1937	George VI Proof from set, see main section.			

Threepences (Brass Type)

Date	Type	Peck	Rarity	Value (AFDC-FDC)
Proofs are all of the standard alloy, as used for the circulation pieces unless otherwise stated.				
1937	George VI Proof from set, see Main section.			
1937	Nickel trial	P2171*	Unique?	£350+ ??
1938	Proof	P2373	Excessively Rare	£350+ ??
1939	Proof	P2375	Excessively Rare	£350+ ??
1940	Proof	P2376	Excessively Rare	£350+ ??
1941	Proof	P2379	Excessively Rare	£350+ ??
1942	Proof	P2381	Excessively Rare	£350+ ??
1943	Proof	P2383	Excessively Rare	£350+ ??
1944	Proof	P2385	Excessively Rare	£350+ ??
1945	Proof	P2387	Excessively Rare	£350+ ??
1946	Proof	P2389	Excessively Rare	£350+ ??
1948	Proof	P2391A	Excessively Rare	£350+ ??
1949	Proof	P2393	Excessively Rare	£400 ??
1950	George VI Proof from set, see main section.			
1951	George VI Proof from set, see main section.			
1952	Proof	P2399	Excessively Rare	£350+ ??
1953	Elizabeth II Proof from set, see main section.			
1954	Proof	P2493	Excessively Rare	£300+ ??
1955	Proof	P2495	Excessively Rare	£300+ ??
1956	Proof	P2497	Excessively Rare	£300+ ??
1957	Proof	P2499	Excessively Rare	£300+ ??
1958	Proof	P2501	Excessively Rare	£300+ ??
1959	Proof	P2501B	Excessively Rare	£300+ ??
1960	Proof	P2501D	Excessively Rare	£300+ ??
1961	Proof	P2501F	Excessively Rare	£300+ ??
1962	Proof	P2501H	Excessively Rare	£300+ ??
1963	Proof	P2501J	Excessively Rare	£300+ ??

Proofs were probably issued for at least the British Museum collection after 1963, but as Peck's book was written in 1963, there are no reference numbers for them.

Coins not intended for circulation - Groats (Fourpences)

Date	Type	ESC	Rarity	Value (AFDC-FDC)
Britannia type groats only, are considered non Maundy.				
1836	Milled edge Proof	1919	Very Rare	£350 ??
1836	Plain edge Proof	1920	Rare	£350 ??
1836	Gold Proof	1921	Excessively Rare	£4000 (1999)
1836	Proof on thin flan	1921A	Excessively Rare	£600+ ??
1837*	Milled edge Proof	1923	Extremely Rare	£350 ??
1837*	Plain edge Proof	1923A	Extremely Rare	£350 ??

* Both are William IV coins. The 1837 coins below are Victorian. Maundy type Groats can be found in the Maundy section.

Date	Type	ESC	Rarity	Value (AFDC-FDC)
1837	Plain edge Proof	1929	Excessively Rare	£1200
1837	Milled edge Proof	1929A	Excessively Rare	£1200
1838	Plain edge Proof	1931	Extremely Rare	£200+
1839	Plain edge Proof	1933	Rare	£200+
1839	Plain edge Proof. up/down	1933A.	V Rare	£200+
1842	Plain edge Proof	1937	Extremely Rare	£200+
1853	Milled edge Proof	1950	Very Rare	£300+ ??
1853	Plain edge Proof	1951	Extremely Rare	£300+
1857	Milled edge Proof	1954	Excessively Rare	£650+ ??
1862	Plain edge Proof	1955A	Extremely Rare	£550+ ??
1862	Plain edge Proof*	1955B	Extremely Rare	£550+ ??

* ESC 1955B uses the threepence Obv die as used for the later type threepence.

Date	Type	ESC	Rarity	Value (AFDC-FDC)
1862	Milled edge Proof	1955C	Extremely Rare	£550+ ??
1888	Proof	1956A	Extremely Rare	£500+ ??

Sixpences

All Sixpence proofs are of silver/cupro-nickel to the same standard as the currency issue unless otherwise stated.

Date	Type	ESC	Rarity	Value (AFDC-FDC)
1816	Proof	1631A	Extremely Rare	£350+
1816	Gold Proof	1631	Excessively Rare	£7000 approx ??
1817	Plain edge Proof	1633	Very Rare	£400+
1817	Milled edge Proof	1633	Extremely Rare	£600
1818	Proof	1635	Extremely Rare	£750
1819	Proof 9/8 in date	1636B	Very Rare	£450
1819	Proof	1637	Very Rare	
1820	Proof (George III)	1639	Very Rare	
1820	Pattern/Proof (George IV)	1653	Excessively Rare	£750+
1821	Proof	1655	Very Rare	£500
1824	Proof	1658	Very Rare	
1825	Proof	1659A	Very Rare	
1826	Proof 2nd Rev	1661	Very Rare	£300 ??
1826	Proof 3rd Rev from set	1663	Rare	£200+ ??
1826	Pewter Proof 3rd Rev	1663A	Extremely Rare	
1829	Proof	1667	Very Rare	
1831	Proof	1671	Very Rare	£400
1831	Plain edge Proof	1672	Rare	£200
1831	Proof on thin flan	1672A	Excessively Rare	
1831	Palladium Proof	1673	Excessively Rare	£1500
1834	Proof	1674B	Extremely Rare	
1834	Proof with round-topped '3'	1675	Extremely Rare	
1835	Proof (Round '3')	1677	Excessively Rare	

Coins not intended for circulation - Sixpences (continued)

Date	Type	ESC	Rarity	Value (AFDC-FDC)
1836	Proof (Round '3')	1679	Excessively Rare	
1837	Proof	1681	Excessively Rare	
1838	Proof	1683	Extremely Rare	£700
1839	Plain edge Proof	1685	Extremely Rare	£300+
	Noted:		An AVF circulated example - £125 (2005)	
1853	Proof	1699	Very Rare	£400
1855	Proof	1701B	Very Rare	£600
1858	Proof	1797	Extremely Rare	£600
1867	Proof	1718	Extremely Rare	£500
1869	Proof	1720A	Extremely Rare	£600
1870	Plain edge Proof	1722	Extremely Rare	£500
1871	Plain edge Proof	1723A	Extremely Rare	£800+
1871	Proof, no die number	1725	Excessively Rare	£500
1878	Proof	1734	Extremely Rare	£450
1879	Milled edge Proof	1737A	Extremely Rare	£400
1879	Plain edge Proof	1737B	Extremely Rare	£600
1880	Proof using rev die of 1839	1738.	Extremely Rare	
1880	Proof	1739	Extremely Rare	£300
1881	Milled edge Proof	1741	Extremely Rare	£500+
1881	Plain edge Proof	1742	Extremely Rare	£600+
1885	Proof	1747	Excessively Rare	£500
1886	Proof	1749	Excessively Rare	£300
1887	Proof (Young Head)	1751	Extremely Rare	£400+
1887	Jubilee head Proof from set, see main section.			
1887	Proof (2nd Rev)	1755	Extremely Rare	£200
1888	Proof	1756A	Excessively Rare	£400
1890	Proof	1758A	Extremely Rare	£300
1893	Proof	1763	Scarce	£70
1902	Matt Proof from set, see main section.			
1911	Proof from set, see main section.			
1921	Proof	ND	?	£495 (2003)
1926	Nickel Proof	1815A	Excessively Rare	£450+
1927	Proof from set, see main section.			
1927	Matt Proof	1816A	Excessively Rare	
VIP proofs exist for most George V dates from 1928 onwards, noted are:				
1931	Proof	ND	Excessively Rare	£300+ ??
1933	Proof	ND	Excessively Rare	£300+ ??
1937	George VI Proof from set, see main section.			
1937	Matt Proof (George VI)	ND	Excessively Rare	
1939	VIP Proof	ND	Extremely Rare	£250
1943	VIP Proof	ND	Extremely Rare	£300
VIP proofs exist for most George VI dates, all are at least extremely rare.				
1946	Cu Ni Proof/Pattern	1836A	Excessively Rare	£400+
1950	Proof from set, see main section.			
1951	Proof from set, see main section.			
1952	Proof	ND	Excessively Rare	£750+
1953	Proof from set, see main section.			
VIP proofs exist for most Elizabeth II dates, all are at least extremely rare.				
1970	Proof from set, see main section.			

Coins not intended for circulation - Shillings

Date	Type	ESC	Rarity	Value (AFDC-FDC)
The coins below are all struck in the same alloy as the circulation coin with a milled edge, unless stated otherwise.				
1816	Gold Proof	1230	Excessively Rare	£9000+ ??
1816	Milled edge Proof	1229	Extremely Rare	£700+ ??
1616	Plain edge Proof	1231	Extremely Rare	£700+ ??
1817	Plain edge Proof	1233	Very Rare	£600+ ??
1820	Proof (George III)	1237	Very Rare	£350+ ??
1820	Proof/Pattern (George IV)	1246	Excessively Rare	£3000 - £4000 ??
1821	Proof	1248	Extremely Rare	£600 ??
1823	Proof	1250	Extremely Rare	£800 ??
1824	Proof	1252	Extremely Rare	£450 ??
1825	Proof (Shield Rev)	1253A	Extremely Rare	£450 ??
1825	Proof*	1255	Rare	£500
1825	Bartons metal Proof*	1256	Extremely Rare	£900 ??
* Both with Lion reverse.				
1826	Proof	1258	Rare	£400
1829	Proof	1261	Extremely Rare	£900 ??
1831	Proof	1266	Rare	£700 ??
1834	Proof	1269	Very Rare	£600+ ??
1835	Proof (Round top '3')	1272	Extremely Rare	£700+ ??
1836	Proof (Round top '3')	1274	Extremely Rare	£700+ ??
1836	Copper Proof	1275	Excessively Rare	£700+ ??
1837	Proof	1277	Very Rare	£700+
1838	Proof	1278	Extremely Rare	£600+
1839	Plain edge Proof (1st head)	1281	Very Rare	£250+
1839	Plain edge Proof (2nd head)	1282	Rare	£350+
1839	Plain edge Proof (3rd head)	1284	Rare	
1839	Proof (3rd head)	1284A	Excessively Rare	
1840	Proof	1286	Extremely Rare	£500 ??
1853	Proof	1301	Very Rare	£500+
1867	Proof	1317	Extremely Rare	£500+
1867	Plain edge Proof	1317A	Extremely Rare	£700+
1871	Proof	1322	Extremely Rare	£500 ??
1871	Plain edge Proof	1323	Excessively Rare	
1878	Proof	1331	Excessively Rare	
1879	Proof	1333	Extremely Rare	£500 ??
1880	Proof	1336	Extremely Rare	£500 ??
1880	Plain edge Proof	1337	Extremely Rare	£500 ??
1881	Proof	1339	Extremely Rare	£500 ??
1881	Plain edge Proof	1340	Excessively Rare	
1884	Proof	1344	Extremely Rare	£500 ??
1885	Proof	1346	Extremely Rare	£500 ??
1886	Proof	1348	Excessively Rare	
1887	Proof (Young Head)	1350	Extremely Rare	£500 ??
1887	Proof from set, see main section.				
1889	Proof	1356	Extremely Rare	£500 ??
The coins below are all struck in the same alloy as the circulation coin with a milled edge, unless stated otherwise.				
1902	Matt Proof from set, see main section.				
1911	Proof from set, see main section.				
1923	Trial piece in Nickel	1433A	Extremely Rare	£400+

Coins not intended for circulation - Shillings (continued)

Date	Type	ESC	Rarity	Value (AFDC-FDC)
1924	Trial piece in Nickel	1434A	Extremely Rare	£400+
1925	Trial in piece Nickel	1449A	Very Rare	£400 ??
1927	Proof from set, see main section.			
1927	Matt Proof	1440A	Excessively Rare	
1937	Proofs from set, see main section.			

VIP Proofs exist for most George VI and Elizabeth II dates. All are extremely rare.

Date	Type	ESC	Rarity	Value (AFDC-FDC)
1946E	Cu-Ni Proof/Pattern	1470A	Excessively Rare	£750+
1950	Proofs from set, see main section.			
1951	Proofs from set, see main section.			
1952	Proof	1475*	Excessively Rare	£8000

* The asterix is part of the ESC number!

Date	Type	ESC	Rarity	Value (AFDC-FDC)
1953	Proofs from set, see main section.			
1958S	Noted VIP Proof	ND	Extremely Rare	£375
1961E	Noted VIP Proof	ND	Extremely Rare	£350+ ??
1961S	Noted VIP Proof	ND	Extremely Rare	£350+ ??
1970	Proofs from set, see main section.			

Eighteen Pences

Date	Type	ESC	Rarity	Value (AFDC-FDC)
1811	Proof	970	Rare	
1812	Proof	973	Rare	
1812	Platinum Proof	974	Excessively Rare	
1812	Small lettering Proof	975	Excessively Rare	
1813	Platinum Proof	976A	Excessively Rare	

Florins

Date	Type	ESC	Rarity	Value (AFDC-FDC)
1851	Proof	804	Extremely Rare	£800+ ??
1852	Proof	807	Very Rare	£800+ ??
1853	Proof	809	Very Rare	£800+
1857	Proof	815	Extremely Rare	£800+ ??
1858	Proof	816A	Extremely Rare	£800+ ??
1862	Plain edge Proof	821	Extremely Rare	£800+ ??
1863	Plain edge Proof	823	Extremely Rare	£800+ ??
1864	Proof on thicker flan	825	Extremely Rare	£800+ ??
1867	Proof (BRITT)*	831	Extremely Rare	£800+ ??
1867	Plain edge Proof (BRITT)*	832	Extremely Rare	£800+ ??

* Legend reads BRITT, as opposed to BRIT on earlier Gothic florins.

Date	Type	ESC	Rarity	Value (AFDC-FDC)
1869	Proof	835	Extremely Rare	£800+ ??
1870	Proof	836A	Extremely Rare	£800+ ??
1871	Proof	838	Extremely Rare	£800+ ??
1871	Plain edge Proof	839	Extremely Rare	£800+ ??

The coins below are all struck in the same alloy as the circulation coin with a milled edge, unless stated otherwise.

Date	Type	ESC	Rarity	Value (AFDC-FDC)
1873	Proof	842	Extremely Rare	£800+ ??
1878	Proof	849B	Excessively Rare	£1000+ ??
1879	Proof	853	Extremely Rare	£800+ ??
1879	Plain edge Proof	853A	Extremely Rare	£800+ ??
1880	Proof	855	Extremely Rare	£800+ ??
1881	Proof	857	Extremely Rare	£800+ ??

Coins not intended for circulation - Florins (continued)

Date	Type	ESC	Rarity	Value (AFDC-FDC)
1881	Plain edge Proof	858	Excessively Rare	£1000+ ??
1885	Proof	862	Excessively Rare	£1000+ ??
1886	Proof	864	Excessively Rare	£1000+ ??
1887	Proof (Gothic)	867	Excessively Rare	£1000+ ??
1887	Jubilee head Proof from set, see main section.			
1892	Proof	875	Excessively Rare	£1000+ ??
1893	Proof	877	Scarce	£150
1902	Matt Proof from set, see main section.			
1911	Proof from set, see main section.			
1922	Gold Proof	941A	Excessively Rare	
1927	Proof from set, see main section.			
VIP proofs of most florins from 1927 until 1963 exist, all are extremely rare.				
1937	Proof from set, see main section.			
1937	Matt proof	957A	Excessively Rare	
1939	Noted VIP Proof	ND	Extremely Rare	£300+ ??
1946	Cu-Ni Proof/trial	966A	Excessively Rare	
1950	Proof from set, see main section.			
1951	Proof from set, see main section.			
1953	Proof from set, see main section.			
1970	Proof from set, see main section.			

Half Crowns

Date	Type	ESC	Rarity	Value (AFDC-FDC)
1816	Proof	614	Very Rare	£1200
1816	Plain edge Proof	615	Very Rare	£1200
1817	Proof	617	Very Rare	£1800
1817	Copper Proof	617A	Excessively Rare	£2000+
1817	Plain edge Proof	617B	Extremely Rare	£1500+
2nd smaller (non Bull type) head from here down.				
1817	Proof	619	Very Rare	£1200+
1817	Plain edge Proof	620	Rare	£1000+
1818	Proof	622	Extremely Rare	£2000
1819	Proof	624	Extremely Rare	£1800
1820	Proof (George III)	626A	Extremely Rare	£2000
1820	Plain edge Proof (GIII)	626	Very Rare	£1500+
1820	Proof (George IV)	629	Very Rare	£1000+
1820	Plain edge Proof (GIV)	630	Extremely Rare	£1500+
1822	Proof/Pattern?	650?	Excessively Rare	£4000+ ??
1821	Proof	632	Very Rare	£1900
1823	Proof (2nd Rev)	635	Extremely Rare	£1600+
1824	Proof	637	Extremely Rare	£1200+ ??
1824	Copper Proof	638	Extremely Rare	£1200+ ??
3rd Reverse, 2nd head from here down.				
1824	Proof/Pattern	639A	Extremely Rare	£1200+ ??
1824	Plain edge Proof/Pattern	639B	Extremely Rare	£1200+ ??
1824	Gold Proof/Pattern	640	Excessively Rare	
1824	Copper Proof/Pattern	641	Extremely Rare	£1000+ ??
1825	Proof	643	Rare	£800
1825	Plain edge Proof	644	Very Rare	£1000
1825	Bartons metal Proof	645	Extremely Rare	£2000
1826	Proof	647	Rare	£475 (EF)

Coins not intended for circulation - Half Crowns (continued)

Date	Type	ESC	Rarity	Value (AFDC-FDC)
1831	Proof (block type WW and plain edge)	657	Rare	£1000
1831	Proof (script WW and plain edge)	658	Rare	
1831	As above, Milled edge	659	Very Rare	
1834	Proof (block WW)	661	Very Rare	£1500+
1834	Proof (script WW)	663	Very Rare	£1000+
1834	Plain edge Proof	664	Extremely Rare	£3000+
1836	Plain edge Proof	666B	Extremely Rare	
1839	Proof type 1	669	Extremely Rare	£2500+
1839	Plain edge Proof type 1	670	Rare	£1400
1839	Plain edge Proof type 2	671	Very Rare	£1500+
1839	Plain edge Proof type 3	671A	Extremely Rare	£3500
1839	Proof type 3, incuse WW	672A	Extremely Rare	£1500+
1839	As above Plain edge	672B	Extremely Rare	£4500

The bust types can be distinguished from the hair ties on the Queen's head. Type 1 = 1 plain and 1 ornate tie. Type 2 = 2 ornate ties. Type 3 = 2 plain ties.

Date	Type	ESC	Rarity	Value (AFDC-FDC)
1850	Proof	685	Extremely Rare	£2200
1851	Proof ??	686 ??	Exists ?	
1852	Proof	687	Very Rare	£1200
1862	Proof	688	Extremely Rare	£2500+
1862	Plain edge Proof	689	Very Rare	£2500+
1864	Proof	690	Very Rare	£2600
1864	Plain edge Proof	691	Very Rare	£2700
1874	Proof	693	Very Rare	
1874	Plain edge Proof	694	Extremely Rare	£2000+ ??
1874	Gold Proof	695	Excessively Rare	
1875	Proof	697	Extremely Rare	£2000+ ??
1875	Plain edge Proof/Pattern	698	Excessively Rare	
1878	Proof	702	Extremely Rare	£2400
1879	Proof	704	Extremely Rare	£2000+ ??
1879	Plain edge Proof	704A	Extremely Rare	£2000+ ??
1880	Proof	706	Extremely Rare	£2000+ ??
1881	Proof	708	Extremely Rare	£2000+ ??
1881	Plain edge Proof	709	Excessively Rare	
1885	Proof	714	Extremely Rare	£1200
1886	Proof	716	Excessively Rare	
1887	Proof (Young head)	718	Extremely Rare	£2000
1887	Jubilee head Proof from set, see main section.			
1893	Proof from set, see main section.			
1902	Proof from set, see main section.			
1911	Proof from set, see main section.			
1924	Matt Proof		Very Rare	£800
1927	Proof from set, see main section.			

VIP Proofs exist for many dates from 1928 - 1963, all are extremely rare.

Date	Type	ESC	Rarity	Value (AFDC-FDC)
1927	Matt Proof	776A	Excessively Rare	
1937	Proof from set, see main section.			
1937	Matt Proof	787A		Excessively Rare
1946	Cu-Ni Proof/Pattern	796A		Excessively Rare
1950	Proof from set, see main section.			
1951	Proof from set, see main section.			
1953	Proof from set, see main section.			
1970	Proof from set, see main section.			

Proof strikings of the 1920's to 1960's halfcrowns range from £300 - £500

Coins not intended for circulation -
Three Shilling - Bank of England Tokens

Date	Type	ESC	Rarity	Value (AFDC-FDC)
1811	Proof, many varieties	At least	Very Rare	£600+
1812	Proof	417	Rare	£500+
1812	Gold Proof	418	Excessively Rare	£9000 ??
1812	Platinum Proof	420	Excessively Rare	£6500+

Double Florins

Date	Type	ESC	Rarity	Value (AFDC-FDC)
1887	Proof [Roman 1]	394	Very Rare	
1887	Proof [Arabic 1]	396	Scarce	

Pattern Double florins also exist for George V and George VI. There are also lots of modern fantasy pieces around. The reader is referred to ESC.

Dollars - Bank of England 5 Shilling Tokens

Date	Type	ESC	Rarity	Value (AFDC-FDC)
1804	Proofs in silver, silver gilt and copper exist. All are Very Rare - Extremely Rare. Values are £600+ for most			

types. The reader is referred to ESC or the 'Nineteenth Century Token Coinage' by W J Davies.

Crowns

Date	Type	ESC	Rarity	Value (AFDC-FDC)
1818	Proof	212	Very Rare	£1000+
1818	Edge inscribed 'Pattern'	213	Excessively Rare	
1819	Proof	217	Very Rare	£1000+
1819	Plain edge Proof	218	Excessively Rare	£3500+ ??
1820	Proof [George III]	220	Extremely Rare	£1000+
1821	Proof	247	Rare	£2000
1821	Copper Proof	248	Excessively Rare	
1821	Copper Proof with plain edge,	249	Excessively Rare	
1821	Proof TERTIO and error edge.	250	Extremely Rare	£3800
1822	Proof [SECUNDO]	251A	Extremely Rare	£3750
1822	Proof [TERTIO]	253	Rare	£2500
1823	Plain edge Proof	254	Excessively Rare	£6000 [asking]
1823	White metal Proof	254A	Excessively Rare	
1825	Plain edge Pattern	255	Extremely Rare	£5000+
1825	As above, in Bartons metal	256	Excessively Rare	
1826	Proof	257	Rare	£2250
1826	Plain edge Proof	258	Excessively Rare	
1826	Proof error LVIII edge	258A	Excessively Rare	
1826	Copper Pattern no edge date	258B	Excessively Rare	
1831	Plain edge Proof / Pattern	271	Very Rare	£2750
1831	Gold Proof / Pattern	272	Extremely Rare	£60,000 [sold??]
1831	Proof / Pattern with W. Wyon signature,	273	Extremely Rare	£6500
1832	Lead Proof	274	Excessively Rare	
1834	Plain edge Proof	275	Extremely Rare	£11,000
1839	Plain edge Proof	279	Rare	£6000
1844	Proof	280A	Excessively Rare	£7500
1845	Proof	283	Excessively Rare	
1847	Milled edge Trial [YH]	287	Excessively Rare	

Coins not intended for circulation - Crowns (continued)

Date	Type	ESC	Rarity	Value (AFDC-FDC)
	Gothic type below this point.			
1847	Proof standard issue	288	Scarce	VF: £700, EF: £1000
1847	Proof SEPTIMO edge	290	Excessively Rare	
1847	Plain edge Proof	291	Rare	£1800
1847	Pure silver VIP Proof	291A	Excessively Rare	£4200
1847	Gold VIP Proof	292	Excessively Rare	£113,000 (in 1988)
1847	White Metal VIP Proof	292A	Excessively Rare	
1853	Proof from set	293	Very Rare	£6500
1853	Plain edge Proof	294	Extremely Rare	£6000
1879	Young Head Proof	295	Excessively Rare	£15,000+
1887	Jubilee head Proof from set, see main section.			
1893	Old head Proof from set, see main section.			
1902	Edward VII Proof from set, see main section.			
1927	Proof from set, see main section.			
1927	Matt Proof	367A	Excessively Rare	
	Proofs exist of all Wreath Crown dates, all are at least		Extremely Rare.	
1934	Proof, noted	ND	Excessively Rare	£4500
1935	Sterling silver Proof	377	Extremely Rare	
1935	.500 Silver Proof	377A	Excessively Rare	£2000
1935	Raised edge Proof	378	Scarce	£250 - £500
1935	Gold Proof	379	Extremely Rare	£18,000
1935	*Error edge Proof	380	Extremely Rare	£3000
	*Correct edge lettering is: DECUS ET TUTAMEN ANNO REGNI XXV			
1937	George VI Proof from set, see main section.			
1937	Frosted Proof	393A	Extremely Rare	
1937	Matt Proof	393B	Excessively Rare	
1951	Frosted Proof	393D	Extremely Rare	£1000+
1951	Sandblasted Proof	393E	Excessively Rare	
1953	Proof from set, see main section.			
1953	Frosted Proof	393H	Extremely Rare	£500+
1953	Sandblasted Proof	393J	Excessively Rare	£500+
1960	VIP Frosted Proof	393M	Extremely Rare	£500+ ??
1965	Satin Finish	393O	Excessively Rare	£800

Below: The beautiful Gothic type crown of 1847.

Coins not intended for circulation - Proof and Uncirculated Sets

Prices quoted are for sets in well preserved cases of issue.

1826	Farthing - £5 coin	(11 coins)	Very Rare	£22,000+
1826	As above with 4 maundy coins.		Very Rare	£20,000+
1831	Farthing - £2 coin	(14 coins)	Very Rare	£16,500+
1839	Farthing - £5 coin	(15 coins)	Very Rare	£27,000+
1853	Half Farthing to 5s	(16 coins)	Very Rare	£27,000+
1887	3d to £5 coin. Jubilee head	(11 coins)	Very Rare	£5,500+
1887	3d to Crown	(7 coins)	Rare	£1000+
1893	3d to £5 coin	(10 coins)	Very Rare	£6,200
1893	3d to Crown	(6 coins)	Rare	£1200+
1902	Maundy 1d - £5 coin	(13 coins)	Scarce (matte)	£1500
1902	Maundy 1d - Sovereign	(11 coins)	Scarce	£550
1911	Maundy 1d - £5 coin	(13)	Scarce	£2,700
1911	Maundy 1d - Sovereign	(11 coins)	Scarce	£1000
1911	Maundy 1d - Half Crown	(8 coins)	Scarce	£425+
1927	3d to Crown	(6 coins)	Scarce	£300
1937	Half Sovereign - £5	(4 coins)	Rare	£2100
1937	Farthing - Crown & Maundy	(15 coins)	Common	£165
1950	Farthing - Half Crown	(9 coins)	Scarce	£75
1951	Farthing - Crown	(10 coins)	Scarce	£100
1953	Farthing - Crown	(10 coins)	Scarce	£70+
1953	Farthing - Half Crown	(9 uncirculated coins)	Common	£20
1968/71	Blue folder 'last decimal set'		Very Common	£1-£3
1970	Half Penny - Halfcrown	(8 coins)	Very Common	£12-£18

Decimal proof sets are in the decimal section.

Complete Maundy Sets (1, 2, 3 and Fourpence coins)

Date	ESC	VF	EF	UNC/BU

GEORGE III .925 fine silver.
4 coins of 12mm, 14mm, 18mm and 19.5mm

Date	ESC	VF	EF	UNC/BU
1800	2421	£30	£130	£170/

Coins now smaller:11mm, 13mm, 16mm and 18mm

1817	2422	£50	£150	£200/
1818	2423	£50	£150	£200/
1820	2424	£50	£150	£200/

GEORGE IV .925 fine silver.
4 coins of 11mm, 13mm, 16mm and 18mm

1822	2425	£30	£100	£150/
1822	2426	Proof set		/£600
1823	2427	£25	£100	£150/
1824	2428	£30	£100	£150/
1825	2429	£25	£80	£100/
1826	2430	£25	£80	£100/
1827	2431	£25	£100	£150/
1828	2432	£25	£80	£100/
1828	2433	Proof set		/£750
1829	2434	£25	£80	£100/
1830	2435	£25	£100	£150/

WILLIAM IV .925 fine silver.
4 coins of 11mm, 13mm, 16mm and 18mm

1831	2436	£35	£95	£175/
1831	2437	Proof set		£250/£450
1831	2438	Proofs in gold		/£15,000
1832	2439	£35	£90	£120/
1833	2440	£35	£95	£120/
1834	2441	£35	£95	£130/
1835	2442	£35	£95	£120/
1836	2443	£40	£100	£175/
1837	2444	£40	£100	£175/

VICTORIA Young Head .925 fine silver.
4 coins of 11mm, 13mm, 16mm and 18mm

1838	2445		£60	£100/
1838	2446	Proof set		£200/
1838	2447	Proofs in gold		/£15,000
1839	2448		£70	£100/

Date	ESC		EF	UNC/BU

VICTORIA (continued)

1839	2449	Proof set		£275/
1840	2450		£70	£100/
1841	2451		£70	£130/
1842	2452		£70	£100/
1843	2453		£70	£100/
1844	2454		£70	£100/
1845	2455		£70	£100/
1846	2456		£75	£100/
1847	2457		£65	£90/
1848	2458		£65	£100/
1849	2459		£75	£110/
1850	2460		£45	£80/
1851	2461		£45	£80/
1852	2462		£50	£90/
1853	2463		£45	£80/
1853	2464	Proof set	£350/£500
1854	2465		£50	£80/
1855	2466		£50	£80/
1856	2467		£50	£80/
1857	2468		£50	£80/
1858	2469		£50	£80/
1859	2470		£50	£80/
1860	2471		£50	£80/
1861	2472		£50	£80/
1862	2473		£50	£80/
1863	2474		£50	£80/
1864	2475		£50	£80/
1865	2476		£50	£80/
1866	2477		£50	£80/
1867	2478		£50	£80/
1867	2479	Proof set		£265/
1868	2480		£50	£80/
1869	2481		£50	£80/
1870	2482		£40	£80/
1871	2483		£40	£80/
1871	2484	Proof set		£500/
1872	2485		£40	£75/
1873	2486		£40	£75/
1874	2487		£40	£75/
1875	2488		£40	£75/
1876	2489		£40	£75/
1877	2490		£40	£75/
1878	2491		£40	£75/
1878	2492	Proofs	£50	£200/

Date	ESC	EF	UNC/BU
VICTORIA (continued)			
Young Head .925 fine silver.			
4 coins of 11mm, 13mm, 16mm and 18mm			
1879	2493	£40	£100/
1879	ND Proofs		£1,000
1880	2494	£40	£100/
1881	2495	£40	£100/
1881	2495A Proofs		£200+/
1882	2496	£40	£100/
1883	2497	£40	£100/
1884	2498	£50	£100/
1885	2499	£40	£100/
1886	2500	£40	£100/
1887	2501	£45	£70/
Jubilee Head			
1888	2502	£40	£75/
1888	2503 Proofs	?	?
1889	2504	£45	£75/
1890	2505	£45	£70/
1891	2506	£45	£70/
1892	2507	£45	£70/
Old/Widow Head			
1893	2508	£45	£80/
1894	2509	£45	£80/
1895	2510	£45	£80/
1896	2511	£45	£80/
1897	2512	£45	£80/
1898	2513	£50	£85/
1899	2514	£40	£85/
1900	2515	£50	£90/
1901	2516	£30	£70/
EDWARD VII types the same.			
1902	2517	£40	£70/
1902	2518 Matt Proofs		/£90
1903	2519	£40	£70/
1904	2520	£40	£70/
1905	2521	£40	£70/
1906	2522	£40	£70/
1907	2523	£40	£70/
1908	2524	£40	£70/
1909	2525	£45	£70/
1910	2526	£50	£70/
GEORGE V types as Edward VII, .500 silver from 1921.			
1911	2527	£30	£55/£70
1911	2528 Proof set		/£60

Date	ESC	EF	UNC/BU
GEORGE V (continued)			
1912	2529	£40	£60/£80
1913	2530	£40	£60/£75
1914	2531	£40	£60/£75
1915	2532	£40	£60/£75
1916	2533	£40	£55/£70
1917	2534	£40	£55/£70
1918	2535	£40	£55/£70
1919	2536	£40	£55/£70
1920	2537	£40	£55/£70
1921	2538	£40	£55/£70
1922	2539	£45	£60/£75
1923	2540	£40	£55/£70
1924	2541	£40	£55/£70
1925	2542	£40	£55/£70
1926	2543	£40	£55/£70
1927	2544	£40	£55/£70
1928	2545	£40	£55/£70
1929	2546	£40	£55/£70
1930	2547	£40	£55/£70
1931	2548	£40	£55/£70
1932	2549	£40	£55/£70
1933	2550	£40	£55/£70
1934	2551	£40	£55/£70
1935	2552	£40	£55/£70
1936	2553	£40	£60/£75
GEORGE VI types as above, .500 silver.			
1937	2554		£50/£65
1938	2555		£60/£75
1939	2556		£60/£75
1940	2557		£60/£75
1941	2558		£60/£75
1942	2559		£60/£75
1943	2560		£60/£75
1944	2561		£60/£75
1945	2562		£60/£75
1946	2563		£60/£75
Silver reverted to .925 Fine.			
1947	2564		£60/£75
1948	2565		£60/£75
1949	2566		£60/£75
1950	2567		£60/£75
1951	2568		£60/£75
1952	2569		£60/£75

Original documentation adds value.
Add £10 - £15 for a set housed in
contemporary dated case.

Date	ESC		UNC/BU	Date	ESC	UNC/BU
ELIZABETH II .925 fine silver.				1977		£60/£80
4 coins of 11mm, 13mm, 16mm & 18mm				1978		£60/£80
1953	1,025		£300/£420	1979		£60/£80
1953	In gold	(1985)	£5,750	1980		£60/£80
1954			£55/£70	1981		£60/£80
1955			£55/£70	1982		£60/£80
1956			£55/£70	1933		£60/£80
1957			£55/£70	1984		£60/£80
1958			£50/£65	1985		£60/£80
1959			£55/£70	1986		£60/£80
1960			£55/£70	1987		£60/£80
1961			£55/£70	1988		£60/£80
1962			£55/£70	1989		£60/£80
1963			£55/£70	1990		£60/£80
1964			£55/£70	1991		£60/£80
1965			£55/£70	1992		£60/£80
1966			£60/£75	1993		£60/£80
1967			£60/£75	1994		£75/£85
1968			£60/£75	1995		£75/£85
1969			£60/£75	1996		£75/£85
1970			£55/£70	1997		£80/£95
Now Decimal pence.				1998		£80/£95
1971			£60/£80	1999		£80/£95
1972			£60/£80	2000		£80/£95
1973			£60/£80	2001		/£100
1974			£60/£80	2002		/£100
1975			£60/£80	2003		/£120
1976			£60/£80	2004 - 2008		-

Left: George III 1800 maundy set. The last set before the current sizes were adopted in 1817. Below: 1882 Victoria maundy set. The reverse types have remained very similar ever since.

Victoria 1898 Maundy Groat

Maundy obverses usually use the same bust as the circulation coinage. With the exception that the laureate George IV bust was used for all George IV maundy money and the first Elizabeth II bust has been, and is still being used for all Elizabeth II maundy money.

Maundy Singles

It's generally preferred to collect complete maundy sets rather than try to obtain each date individually, mainly because individual coins can be difficult to track down of certain dates, and it can often work out more expensive. Also, complete sets tend to all have the same toning, and they therefore match better. Individual coins do often appear for sale with prices varying greatly. Below is a list of approximate prices for coins in Uncirculated condition:

George III	UNC
1800 set	
Fourpence	£30 - £50
Threepence	£30 - £50
Twopence	£25 - £40
Penny	
£25 - £35	
1817 - 1820 type	
Fourpence	£30 - £40
Threepence	£30 - £40
Twopence	£20 - £30
Penny	
£20 - £30	
George IV	
Fourpence	£20 - £30
Threepence 1822	£40 - £50
Threepence (others)	£20 - £30
Twopence	£15 - £25
Penny	£15 - £25
William IV	
Fourpence	£20 - £30
Threepence	£30 - £40
Twopence	£20 - £30
Penny	£15 - £25
Victoria	
Young Head (1838 - 1887)	
Fourpence	£20 - £30
Threepence	£35 - £40
Twopence	£15 - £20
Penny	£10 - £15

Victoria (continued)	UNC
Jubilee Head (1888 - 1892)	
Fourpence	£15 - £25
Threepence	£20 - £30
Twopence	£10 - £20
Penny	£10 - £20
Old Head (1893 - 1901)	
Fourpence	£15 - £25
Threepence	£20 - £30
Twopence	£10 - £20
Penny	£10 - £20
Edward VII & George V	
Fourpence	Around £15
Threepence	£15 - £20
Twopence	£10 - £15
Penny	£10 - £15
George VI and Elizabeth II up to 1970	
Fourpence	Around £15
Threepence	Around £15
Twopence	Around £15
Penny	Around £15
Elizabeth II 1971 - 1998	
Fourpence	Around £20
Threepence	Around £20
Twopence	Around £20
Penny	Around £20

More recent maundy sets/singles are not often offered.

Decimal Coinage Section

I'll be the first to admit that the decimal coverage in this book is not as comprehensive as the predecimal coins listed on the previous pages. It's not that I dislike decimals, far from it. The fact of the matter is, I felt that this book should concentrate on the older, generally more collected coinage and that a whole new and separate book, dedicated to decimals would be a good idea.

A complete book containing all the decimal types and known varieties is available from Rotographic. With each coin type illustrated (in colour), it's over 80 pages on its own! The ISBN is 978-0-948964-80-0 and the book is called 'Check Your Change'. Some more details are shown on page 2.

Date	Details	BU / Proof
The Halfpenny - Bronze 17mm		
1971		10p / £2
1971	Double headed	£200 /
1972	Proof Only	/ £5
1973 - 1981	20p / £2	
1982		10p / £2
1983		20p / £2
1984	From set only	£2 / £3
The Penny - Bronze 20.32mm		
1971		10p / £2
1972	Proof Only	/ £5
1973 - 1977	10p / £3	
1978		15p / £2
1979		10p / £2
1980		10p / £2
1981		15p / £2
1982		10p / £2
1983		15p / £2
1984	From set only	50p / £2
1985 - 1991	20p / £2	
1992	From set only (bronze)	£3 / £3

Date	Details	BU / Proof
The Penny (Continued)		
Copper plated steel until 1998		
(magnetic).		
1992		20p / £2
1993		20p / £2
1994		20p / £2
1995		10p / £2
1996		10p / £2
1997		10p / £2
1998		10p / £2
1999		5p / £2
2000		5p / £2
2001		5p / £2
2002		5p / £2
2003		5p / £1
2004		2p / £1
2005		
2006		
2007		

Date	Details	BU/Proof
The Twopence - Bronze 25.9Imm		
1971		10p/£2
1972 - 1974	Proof Only	/£4
1975 - 1981		25p/£2
Legend changed to 'TWO PENCE'		
1982	From set only	£2/£2
1983	From set only	£2/£2
1983	Error. A mule with the old	
	'NEW PENCE' type reverse.	
	From set only	£400/
1984	From set only	£1/£2
1985 - 1991		25p/£2
1992	From set only (bronze)	£2/£2
	Copper plated steel until	
	1998 (magnetic)	
1992 - 1995		25p/£2
1996 - 2002		10p/£2
2003		5p/
2004		Face value/
2005		Face value/
2006		Face value/
2007		Face value/

Date	Details	BU/Proof
The Five Pence - Cupro-Nickel 23.5mm		
1968		20p/
1969		30p/
1970		30p/
1971		30p/£2
1972	Proof Only	/£5
1973	Proof Only	/£5
1974	Proof Only	/£5
1975		30p/£2
1976	Proof Only	30p/£2
1977		30p/£2
1978		30p/£2
1979		30p/£2
1980		20p/£2
1981	Proof Only	/£3
1982	From sets only	£3/£3
1983	From sets only	£3/£3
1984	From sets only	£3/£3
1985	From sets only	£3/£3
1986	From sets only	£3/£3
1987		30p/£2
1988		30p/£2
1989		25p/£2
1990	From sets only	£2/£2

Date	Details	BU/Proof
The Five Pence - (Continued)		
Size reduced to 18mm		
1990	Silver Proof	/£10
1990	Silver Piedfort Proof	/£20
1991		20p/£2
1992		20p/£2
1993	From set only	£1/£2
1994		25p/£2
1995		20p/£2
1996		20p/£2
1996	Silver Proof	/£12
1997		15p/£2
1998		15p/£2
1999		10p/£2
2000		10p/£2
2001		10p/£2
2002		10p/£1
2003		5p/£1
2004		Face value/
2005		Face value/
2006		Face value/
2007		Face value/

Date	Details	BU/Proof
The Ten Pence - Cupro-Nickel 28.5mm		
1968		20p/
1969		30p/
1970		30p/
1971		30p/£2
1972	Proof Only	/£2
1973		30p/£2
1974 - 1979		30p/£2
1980		50p/£2
1981		50p/£2
1982	From set only	£3/£3
1983	From set only	£3/£3
1984	From set only	£3/£3
1985 - 1992	From set only	£3/£3
1992	Silver Proof	/£10
Size now reduced to 24.5mm		
1992		30p/£2
1992	Silver Proof	/£10
1992	Silver Piedfort Proof	/£25
1993	From set only	£2/£2
1994	From set only	£2/£2
1995		30p/£2
1996		30p/£2
1997 - 2002		30p/£2
2003		20p/£1
2004 - 2007		Face value/

Date	Details	BU/Proof
The Twenty Pence - Cupro-Nickel 7 sided, 21.4mm		
1982		50p/£3
1982		/£40
1983 - 1994		50p/£3
1995		40p/£1
1996		40p/£1
1997 - 2002		40p/£1
2003		20p/£2
2004 - 2007		Face value/

Twenty Five Pence - See Decimal Crowns

Date	Details	BU/Proof
The Fifty Pence - Cupro-Nickel 7 sided, 30mm		
1969		£2/£4
1969	Double Heads	£150+?
19??	Double Tail 'New Pence'	£200+?
1970		£3/£4
1971	Proof Only	/£4
1972	Proof Only	/£4
1973	EEC Hands	£2/£3
1973	EEC on Thick blank	£2000
1974	Proof Only	/£4
1975 - 1989	(1975 is proof only)	£2/£4
1990		£3/£6
1991		£4/£5
1992		£4/£5
1993		£4/£4
1992/93	Star Design EEC related	£5/£9
1992/93	EEC Silver Proof	/£15
1992/93	EEC Silver Piedfort Proof	/£40
1992/93	EEC Gold Proof	/£450
1994	D-Day	30p/£2
1994	D-Day Silver Proof	/£30
1994	D-Day Silver Piedfort Proof	/£45
1994	D-Day Gold Proof	/£450
1995	From set only	£2/£4
1996	From set only	30p/
1996	Silver Proof	/£12
1997		£2/£4
Size reduced to 27.3mm		
1997		£2/£3
1998	Normal Reverse	£2/£3
1998	EU Anniversary	£2/£4
1998	EU Silver Proof	/£20
1998	EU Silver Piedfort Proof	/£40
1998	EU Gold Proof	/£300

Date	Details	BU/Proof
The Fifty Pence - (Continued)		

Silver Proof stikings and Piedfort silver Proof strikings are worth around £20 and £40 respectively. * Issue Prices

Date	Details	BU/Proof
1999	Normal Reverse	£2/£3
2000	Public Libraries 150th Anniversary	£3/£3
2000	Normal Reverse	£2/£3
2001	Normal Reverse	£2/£3
2002	Normal Reverse	£2/£3
2003	Suffragette Movement 100th Anniversary	£1/£3
2003	Normal Reverse	£1/£2
2004	Normal Reverse	Face value/
2004	Anniversary of 4 minute mile	Face value/
2004	Piedfort Silver Proof	/£40
2005	Normal Reverse	Face value/
2005	Samuel Johnston	Face value/
2005	S Johnson Silver proof	£26.50*
2005	S Johnson Piedfort Proof	£50.00*
2006	Victoria Cross (2 coins) Pair in folder	£6.95*/
	Silver proof:	
	The Award coin	£27.50*
	Heroic acts coin	£27.50*
2007	Scouting	50p/£1
	Scouting Silver Proof	£30
	Scouting Piedfort Proof	£45
2007	Normal Reverse	50p/£1

The One Pound Coin, Nickel Brass 22.5mm
Every year since the first issue in 1983, the One pound coin is given a new reverse prepresenting a part of the UK. To save space these are not all illustrated in this issue. Coins with the wrong reverse for the year are usually forgeries.

Date	Details	BU/Proof
1983	Coat of Arms - UK	£3/£4
	In wallet/card	£5/
	Cased Silver Proof	/£25
	Piedfort Silver Proof	/£120
1984	Thistle - Scotland	£2/£5
	In wallet/card	£5/
	Cased Silver Proof	/£20
	Piedfort Silver Proof	/£45
1985	Leek reverse - Wales	£3/£5
	In wallet/card	£5/
	Cased Silver Proof	/£20
	Silver Piedfort Proof	/£45

Date	Details	BU / Proof
The One Pound Coin (Continued)		
1986	Flax - N. Ireland	£2/£5
	In wallet/card	£5/
	Cased Silver Proof	/£25
	Piedfort Silver Proof	/£45
1987	Oak Tree - Whole UK	£2/£5
	In wallet/card	£5/
	Cased Silver Proof	/£25
	Piedfort Silver Proof	/£45
1988	Royal Arms Reverse	£3/£5
	In wallet/card	£6/
	Cased Silver Proof	/£28
	Piedfort Silver Proof	/£45
1989	Reverse as 1984	£2/£5
	In wallet/card	£5/
	Cased Silver Proof	/£25
	Piedfort Silver Proof	/£50
1990	Reverse as 1985	£2/£4
	Cased Silver Proof	/£22
1991	Reverse as 1986	£2/£4
	Cased Silver Proof	/£22
1992	Reverse as 1987	£2/£4
	Cased Silver Proof	/£22
1993	Reverse as 1983	£2/£4
	Cased Silver Proof	/£30
	Piedfort Silver Proof	/£50
1994	Scottish single Lion	£2/£5
	In wallet/card	£3
	Cased Silver Proof	/£30
	Piedfort Silver Proof	/£50
1995	Welsh Dragon	£3/£5
	In Welsh wallet/card	£5/
	In English wallet/card	£4/
	Cased Silver Proof	/£25
	Piedfort Silver Proof	/£50
1996	Celtic Cross for N.I.	£2/£4
1997	English 3 Lions	£2/£4
	In wallet/card	£5/
	Cased Silver Proof	/£25
	Piedfort Silver Proof	/£50
1998	Reverse as 1983	£2/£5
	In wallet/card	£3/
	Cased Silver Proof	/£25
	Piedfort Silver Proof	/£45
1999	Reverse as 1994	£2/£5
	In wallet/card	£3/
	Cased Silver Proof	/£25
	Piedfort Silver Proof	/£45
2000	Reverse as 1995	£2/£4
	In wallet/card	£3/
	Cased Silver Proof	/£25
	Piedfort Silver Proof	/£45

Date	Details	BU/Proof
The One Pound Coin (Continued)		
2001	Reverse as 1996	£2/£4
	In wallet/card	£3/
	Cased Silver Proof	/£25
	Piedfort Silver Proof	/£45
2002	Reverse as 1997	£2/£4
	In wallet/card	£3/
	Cased Silver Proof	/£25
	Piedfort Silver Proof	/£45
2003	Reverse as 1983 Face value	/£3
2004	Forth Bridge Face value	/£2
	In wallet/card	£4/
2004	Set of 4 silver Heraldic 'Pattern' Coins. Retail at	/£97.50
2005	Menai bridge Face value	/£2
	Cased Silver Proof, retail	£27.50
	Piedfort Silver Proof, retail	£50
2006	Egyptian Arch	£1/£2
	Cased Silver Proof, retail	£28.50
	Piedfort Silver Proof, retail	£50
2007	Millenium Bridge	£1/£2
	Cased Silver Proof, retail	£28.50
	Piedfort Silver Proof, retail	£50

Date	Details	BU/Proof
The Two Pound Coin - Nickel brass 28.4mm		
1986	Scottish Commonwealth games	£3/£6
	In wallet/card	/£25
	.500 Silver Proof	/£13
	.925 Silver Proof	/£20
	Gold Proof	/£200
1989	Bill of Rights	£3-5/
1989	Claim of Rights	£6-8/
1989	Pack containing both Claim and Bill of rights coins	£10/
1989	Proof of either	/£20
1989	Piedfort Proof Pair	/£75
1994	Bank of England Anniversary	£3/£5
	Cased Silver Proof	/£25
	Piedfort Silver Proof	/£45
	Gold Proof	/£400
	Error. No 'Two pounds' on Obv	/£700
1995	End of WWII. Dove	£3/£5
	Cased Silver Proof	/£25
	Piedfort Silver Proof	/£45
	Gold Proof	/£375
1995	UN Anniversary	£3/£6
	UN Silver Proof	/£25
	UN Piedfort Silver Proof	/£45
	UN Gold Proof	/£350

Date	Details	BU/Proof
The Two Pound Coin - (Continued)		
1996	Europe Football Championship	£3/£5
	Cased Silver Proof	/£25
	Piedfort Silver Proof	/£45
	Gold Proof	/£300

Standard Bi Metallic Issue

1997 - 2000 Normal issue		£3/£6
Where available:		
Silver/gold plated Proof		/£22
Piedfort version		/£45
Two tone Gold Proof		/£325

Commemorative Issues (again)

1999	Rugby World Cup	£3/£6
	Cased Silver Proof	/£22
	Piedfort Silver Proof	/£45
	Two tone Gold Proof	/£325

Date	Details	BU/Proof
The Two Pound Coin (Continued)		
2001	Marconi Commemorative	£3/£
	Cased Silver Proof	/£25
	Piedfort Silver Proof	/£40
	Two tone Gold Proof	/£325
2002	Manchester Commonwealth	
	Games 4 coin set:	£12/£22
	Silver Proof Set	/£75
	Piedfort coloured set	/£50
	Gold Proof single	/£320
	Gold Proof set	/£1000+
2003	DNA discovery	£3/£8
	Cased Silver Proof	/£25
	Piedfort Silver Proof	/£45
	Gold Proof	/£295

Date	Details	BU/Proof
2004	Trevithick Steam train	£3/£5
	Silver striking	£15*/
	Piedfort Silver Proof	/£50*
2005	Normal reverse	£2/£3
2005	WWII	£3/£5
	Silver proof	/£30*
	Piedfort Silver Proof	/£50*
2005	Gunpowder Plot	£3/£5
	Silver proof	/£30*
2006	I.K.Brunel pair (each)	£3/£5
	Pair in pack	£9.95*
	Silver proof:	
	The man	/£29.95*
	His achievements	/£29.95*
2007	Act of Union/Slave Trade (each)	£3/£5
	Silver Proof of either	/£30*
	Silver Piedfort Proof of either	/£50*

* Issue Prices

The Crown and Five Pound Coin - Cupro Nickel 38.6mm
After decimalisation the Crown, when struck had its usual face value of 5 shillings (or 25p in decimal). The face value was changed to £5 in 1990.

Date	Type	BU	Pack*	Proof	Silver P	Gold P
Twenty-Five pence Face value:						
1972	Silver Wedding	£1	£5	£14-£20		
1977	Silver Jubilee	£1	£3	£4	£12-£20	
1980	Queen Mother Birthday	£1	£2	£5	£15-£22	
1981	Charles' Wedding	£1	£2	£5	£20-£25	
Now with Five Pounds face value:						
1990	Queen Mother B'day	£7	£9		£40	£600
1993	Coronation Anniversary	£7	£9	£9	£30	£600
1996	Queens 70th Birthday	£7	£9	£10	£30	£650
1997	Golden Wedding	£7	£9	£10	£30	£600
1998	Charles' Birthday	£7	£9	£10	£30	£600
1999	Diana Commemorative	£7	£9	£10	£30	£600
1999	Millenium	£6	£8	£9	£28	£550
2000	Millenium	£6	£8	£9	£28	£550
	With Dome Mint Mark	£14				
2000	Queen Mother Birthday	£6	£9		£28	£600
	As above, Silver Piedfort Proof				£55	
2001	Victorian Anniversary	£6	£9		£28	£550
2002	Golden Jubilee	£6	£9		£28	£550
2003	Coronation Jubilee	£6	£8		£28	£550
2003	Queen Mother Memorial		£8		£28	£550
2004	Entente Cordiale	£6	£8			
2005	Nelson commemorative	£5	£8		£30	
2005	Trafalgar commemorative	£5	£8		£30	
2005	Pair of 2005 crowns piedfort proofs				£135 issue price	
2006	Queen's 80th Birthday	£5	£10		£40 issue price	
2007	Diamond Wedding	£5	£10		£40 issue price (£80 pied)	

*Pack = In official Royal mint packet. AG = Silver, AU = Gold.

Decimal Proof and Uncirculated Sets

Sets that possess packaging in absolutely mint condition and no toning on the coins are generally more sought after. The Uncirculated sets are often referred to as BU sets. Many sets, especially the earlier ones, often appear for sale at cheaper prices.

Dates	Type	Value
Proof Sets:		
1971-1982	Proof sets in card	Up to £8
1983-1995	Proof sets in leatherette	Up to £12
1996-2003	Proof sets in leatherette	Up to £20
1985-2000	Deluxe Leather Proof sets	£15-£25
2001-2003	Deluxe Leather Proof sets	Up to £30
2000-2003	Executive Proof sets	Up to £60
2004	Proof Set issue price	Around £35
2004	Deluxe Proof set issue price	Around £48
2004	Executive Set issue price	Around £70
2005	Proof Set issue price	Around £35
2005	Deluxe Proof Set issue price	Around £48
2005	Executive Set issue price	Around £75
2006	Executive Set issue price	Around £75
2007	Executive Set issue price	Around £75
Uncirculated (BU) sets:		
1982-1995	Uncirculated sets	£5-£7
1996-2003	1p - £2 Coin BU set (9 coins)	Up to £10
1989-1999	Baby/Boy/Girl/Wedding sets -	£6-£10
2000-2003	Wedding/Baby sets	Up to £15
2004	1p - £2 BU set issue price	Around £15
2004	Wedding/Baby set issue price -	Around £20
2005	1p - £2 BU set issue price	Around £15
2005	Wedding/Baby set issue price -	Around £20
2006	1p - £2 BU set issue price	Around £15
2006	Wedding/Baby set issue price -	Around £20
2007	1p - £2 BU set issue price	Around £15
2007	Wedding/Baby set issue price -	Around £20

A Glossary Numismatic terms and Abbreviations

Many of the abbreviations used in this book are standard Coin collectors jargon, there are however, a few that may not be so obvious. This glossary should clear things up:

Alignment: The relationship between the obverse and reverse of the coin. Either the reverse is up side down compared to the obverse when rotated with fingers at the top and bottom of the coin, or the reverse is up the same way when the coin is rotated with fingers at the top and bottom of the coin. The latter is the most common alignment for British coins dated 1860-date and may be referred to in this book as up/up. In the same way the upside down alignment may sometimes be referred to as up/down.

Berries: Usually refers to the number of berries in the wreath around the monarch's head.

BV: Bullion Value. i.e no collectors premium over the value of the metal.

H: An 'H' after the date in the first column indicates the coin was struck at the Heaton Mint in Birmingham. The 'H' mintmark will appear on the coin either next to, or under its date.

Incuse: Struck inwards. Lettering or a design element on a coin that is the opposite to raised. For example, the edge lettering on the modern £1 coin.

KN: A 'KN' after the date in the first column indicates the coin was struck at the Kings Norton Mint in Birmingham. The 'KN' will appear on the coin next to the date.

Modified Effigy: (George V only) In the absence of a direct comparison, the modified effigy (or modified head) can be distinguished by the initials which appear on the truncation of the neck. Before modification, the initials B.M. are placed near the centre of truncation. After modification they appear, without stops, well to the right thus: BM (not B.M.) The initials are those of the designer of the coin: Bertram Mackennal.

Mule: A Mule is when a coin gets made with the wrong combination of obverse and reverse.

Obverse: (or Obv) The side of the coin with the head of the Monarch on.

Pattern: A proposed coin type that was not used for circulation.

Piedfort: A coin that is struck on a thicker blank than is usual. Relatively recently the Royal mint starting coining Silver Piedfort coins.

Pointing/Points: To distinguish a different die used to strike a particular coin, often 'pointings' are used. They normally refer to a letter or design element on the coin, and to whether it points directly at, or between two border teeth or another element of the coin.

Proof: A special striking of a coin using specially prepared and polished dies and blanks.

Reverse: (or Rev) The opposite side of the coin to the obverse, or the 'tails' side.

Teeth/Beads: The small teeth or circles surrounding the inner rim of many British coins. Beads are circular, teeth are elongated.

Truncation: (or trunc) The base of the monarch's neck, often containing the designers initials.

A Timeline of British / World events from 1797

1798	Income tax set at 10% on incomes over £200 p.a.
1799	Napoleon Bonaparte becomes First Consul in France.
1800	Union of Great Britain and Ireland established.
1801	First national census.
1803	War with France.
1804	Napoleon becomes French Emperor.
1805	Battle of Trafalgar - Nelson defeats Spanish and French fleets.
1807	Slave trade outlawed in Britain and its Empire.
1811	Prince of Wales made Regent due to Kings mental health.
1813	East India company's monopoly abolished.
1814	Paris falls, Napoleon abdicates.
1815	Napoleon returns - Battle of Waterloo takes place.
1820	Death of King George III
1821-23	Great Irish famine.
1825	Unions legalised. Stockton / Darlington railway opened.
1830	Great Reform Bill introduced.
1830	Death of King George IV.
1830	Liverpool / Manchester railway opened.
1830-32	Major Cholera outbreak. Reform Bill becomes law.
1833	Factory act limits child labour. Education act introduced.
1834	Slavery completely abolished.
1835	Municipal Reform Act
1837	Death of King William IV
1839	Chartist riots.
1840	First stamp, the Penny Black intorduced.
1844-45	Irish potato famine begins. 5,000 miles of railway laid.
1848	Public health act.
1851	The Great Exhibition takes place.
1854-56	War with Russia (The Crimean War)
1857-58	Second Opium War opens up China to European trade.
1858	Indian mutiny.
1859	Darwin publishes 'Origin of Species'.
1861	Death of Prince Albert (Queen Victoria's Husband)
1861-65	The American civil war.
1867	Dominion of Canada act.
1869	Opening of Suez canal.
1870	Married women's property right act.
1871	German Empire established from the many independent states.
1876	Victoria proclaimed Empress of India.
1879	Zulu War.
1880-81	First Boer War.
1882	Britain occupies Egypt.
1886	First Irish Home Rule Bill. Gold found in the Transvaal.
1896	Start of German Naval expansion.
1899	Second Boer War begins.
1900	Commonwealth of Australia act. Boxer rising in China.
1901	Death of Queen Victoria.

A Timeline of British / World events from 1797

1902	Education Act. Alliance with Japan.
1904	Anglo-French 'Entente'.
1907	Anglo-Russian 'Entente'.
1908	Old Age Pension plan introduced.
1909	Union of South Africa act.
1910	Death of Edward VII.
1911	National Insurance act.
1912	Talks with Germany over Naval build up.
1914	Assination of Austrian Archduke Franz Ferdinand at Sarajevo.
1914	4th August, British Empire enters the First World War.
1918	11th November, First World War ends after too many deaths.
1919	Treaty of Versailles.
1921	Most Irish counties gain dominion status, to become the 'Irish Free State'.
1922	Mussolini comes to power in Italy.
1926	General Strike.
1931	Financial crisis. Britain abandons the Gold Standard.
1933	Adolf Hitler becomes Chancellor of Germany.
1936	Spanish Civil War. Germany sends 'Condor Legion'.
1936	Death of George V.
1936	Edward VIII abdicates to marry an American divorcee.
1938	Prime Minister Neville Chamberlain meets Adolf Hitler.
1939	Britain guarantees Polish neutrality.
1939	Germany invades Poland. British Empire declares war on Germany.
1940	Winston Churchill becomes Prime Minister.
1940	Invasion prevented in the successful 'Battle of Britain'.
1941	Hitler invades the Soviet Union. Japan bomb Pearl Harbor.
1945	Germany and Japan defeated, Second World War ends.
1945	The UN is founded.
1947	India gains independence from Britain.
1949	NATO founded.
1950	Korean War begins.
1951	The Festival of Britain is held in London.
1952	Death of King George VI.
1957	First satellite launched by Russia.
1961	Russia put the first man into space.
1962	Cuban Missile crisis.
1963	French veto Britains attempt to join European Common Market.
1963	American president John F Kennedy is assassinated.
1965	Winston Churchill dies.
1969	American astronauts land on the moon.
1969	British troops sent to Northern Ireland.
1972	Britain enters the European Economic Community.
1982	Falklands War with Argentina.
1986	Cold war ends, the Soviet Union begins withdrawing troops from Eastern Europe.
1989-90	Berlin wall torn down and Germany re-united.

A Timeline of British/World events from 1797

1992	British troops sent to Bosnia.
1994	South Africa holds first multi-national elections.
1997	Princess Diana killed in Paris car crash.
1998	Good Friday agreement in Northern Ireland.
2000	Dr Harold Shipman sentenced to life in prison.
2001	Planes crash in to World trade centre buildings.
2002	Queen Mother dies.
2003	War in Iraq, Saddam Hussein overthrown.
2004	Bombing in Madrid. Tsunami in Indian Ocean.
2005	Bombings in London. Sein Fein annouces IRA to disband.
2006	The Queen celebrates her 80th Birthday
2007	Hairline fractures in the world economy start to appear!

The following books were used as reference during the writing of this book, and are recommended for further reading:

Previous editions of **"Collectors' Coins Great Britain"**. (most are out of print)

"Collectors' George III Coins", by R J Marles. (out of print)

"The British Bronze Penny", by Michael Gouby.
(Available from the author: www.michaelcoins.co.uk)

"English Copper, Tin and Bronze coins in the British Museum 1558-1958", by C Wilson Peck. (out of print)

"The Bronze Coinage of Great Britain", by Michael J Freeman. (Available new)

"English Silver Coinage since 1649", by P Alan Rayner. (Available new)

"British Silver Coins Since 1816", by Peter J Davies. (Available new)

"Standard Catalog of World Coins", by C L Krause and C Mishler. (Available new, published in the USA)

"A Guide Book of English Coins", by K E Bressett. (Out of print but often available second hand on eBay, published in the USA)

"The Sovereign", by Daniel Feardon / Brian Reeds. (Available new)

Also recommended is: **"The Early British Bronze Bun Penny 1860 - 1865 and their varieties"**, by John Jerrams.

The Cover Coin

The main image on the front of this book is of a 1937 Crown. These crowns are still fairly common coins and their value is not particularly high. Nevertheless, I quite like the coat of arms design on the reverse and being the largest George VI coin, they show off the T H Paget bust of the king in its fullest glory. Incidentally, this coin was the last mass-produced crown to be struck in silver (50% fine) as the next crown in 1951 was cupro-nickel, as were all those that followed until the 5 shilling coin was re-valued as £5 in 1990 and the Royal Mint started issuing silver proof versions. How special a crown must have been in 1937, in the days before one or two different crowns were minted each year to mark the types of special occasions (with commercial appeal) that are rendered no longer special by the sheer frequency with which they seem to occur!

Copyright Notice